WHAT
SCHOOL
LEADERS
NEED TO
KNOW ABOUT
ENGLISH
LEARNERS

BY JAN EDWARDS DORMER

This book has a companion website. Go to www.tesol.org/school-leaders for additional resources.

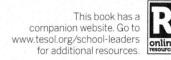

www.tesol.org/bookstore

TESOL International Association
1925 Ballenger Avenue
Alexandria, Virginia 22314 USA
Tel 703-836-0774 • Fax 703-836-7864
www.tesol.org

Director of Publishing: Myrna Jacobs
Cover Design: Citrine Sky Design
Copy Editor: Tomiko Breland
Layout and Design: Capitol Communications, LLC

ISBN 978-1-942799-84-9
Library of Congress Control Number 2016948187

Contents

Chapter 1

How Can a Good Understanding of
English Learning Transform Your School? 1

Chapter 2

What Do You Need to Know About TESOL? 15

Chapter 3

What Does It Mean to "Know English"? 29

Chapter 4

How Does Someone Learn English? 43

Chapter 5

How Does Someone Learn English in School? 67

Chapter 6

Where Can an ELL Best Acquire Language and Learn Content? 87

Professional Development Guide 113

Appendix A: Acronyms in TESOL 125

Appendix B: Home Language Survey 127

CHAPTER 1

How Can a Good Understanding of English Learning Transform Your School?

"Why can't you just call it 'ESL' like everyone else?" complained a teacher in a professional development seminar on teaching English language learners, reacting to my abundant use of the acronym "TESOL." Another teacher piped up, "Well, in our school we call it ELL. I agree—there are too many acronyms, and I don't understand why we can't all just use the same one. It would be a lot less confusing." I am all for reducing confusion, so I explained to these teachers that TESOL[1] (*teaching* English to speakers of other languages) is what teachers do, and an ELL (English language *learner*) is a **student**. ESL (*English* as a second language) is what the student learns—**English**. I even dared to share a new acronym, ESOL (*English* for speakers of other languages), as an alternative to *ESL,* because for many ELLs, English is a third or fourth, not a second, language

Still, I left that seminar feeling uneasy, knowing that I had not adequately addressed the true pressing question: Why does it matter? Are we just learning terminology for the sake of knowing all the right terms in the alphabet soup of TESOL? No. The lack of appropriate, common language for discussing the needs of ELLs is simply a manifestation of the tremendous challenges in educating this exploding population in our schools. According to the National Center for Education Statistics (2014), around 10% of American school children are ELLs, and this percentage is growing each year. In large cities, this number rises to nearly 17%. About half of all immigrants are limited in English proficiency,

---

[1] The term "TESOL" also means "Teachers of English to Speakers of Other Languages" when used to refer to TESOL International Association.

according to the Migration Policy Institute (Zong & Batalova, 2015), and 8% of the total U.S. population over age 5 is classified as limited English proficient (LEP). But the current statistics aren't even the most compelling. Rather, it is the predicted growth in this population that really gives us pause: according to some predictions, ELLs will comprise 50% of the American school population in another 25 years.

And the growth in numbers is only a part of the picture. There is also increasing diversity in the ELL population. In many schools, ELLs now represent a dozen or more native languages and cultures, and virtually every major global region. And the diversity does not end with language and geography. Many schools have among their ELL populations both students coming from world-class preparatory schools in their home countries and those coming from refugee camps, with very little formal education.

Given these realities, it is perhaps not surprising that teachers often place "instruction of ELLs" as their number one professional development need. In some school districts in Pennsylvania, it is rated as twice as urgent as other training needs (Burchard, Dormer, & Fisler, 2015). And Pennsylvania is not unique. (See, for example, the National Clearinghouse for English Language Acquisition, 2011, for more on the growing number of ELLs.) Throughout the United States and around the world, teachers are asking the question: How do I teach students who are not yet proficient in English?

A clear mandate from teachers for more and better preparation is not the only reason a school leader might want to read a book like this one. The lack of understanding of ELLs, of multilingualism, and of multiculturalism can have damaging consequences—not only for the teachers and students involved, but for the school. For example, what happens when uninformed teachers make statements or engage in actions that are perceived as threatening or discriminatory to immigrant families or international students? And what is the result of ELLs spending a majority of their school time in high stress conditions due to a pervasive lack of understanding of the realities of language acquisition? And what about the potential for linguistic, racial, and ethnic divisions in schools when a culture embracing diversity is not fostered? Beyond our need and desire to truly *educate* ELLs lies the very real potential for legal and safety problems if we do not. But beyond legal, safety, and compliance issues, we find the most compelling reason for embracing the ELLs in our schools: the richness that they bring. The linguistic skills, diverse life experiences, and multicultural perspectives that ELLs bring to our schools are priceless, as we will see throughout the remainder of this chapter and book.

This chapter introduces three key steps that school leaders can take to ensure that the needs of teachers, ELLs, and indeed all learners are well met in their schools: 1) fostering a school culture that values and welcomes multiple languages and cultures; 2) ensuring that all teachers have the necessary knowledge, skills, and abilities to meet the needs of ELLs, especially given changing teacher roles as a result of the Common Core State Standards (CCSS); and 3) creating school schedules conducive to meeting ELL needs.

▪ ▪ ▪ Fostering a School Culture That Values and Welcomes Multiple Languages and Cultures

The ability to speak more than one language is something that we would all say we value. The fact that foreign language classes are a regular part of a high school curriculum affirms this value, as does the fact that foreign languages and global awareness are identified as 21st-century skills. We also know that bilingual individuals outperform monolinguals in a number of ways. However, our language practices and policies often tell a different story. They often send a strong message that only English should be used in school. Often, even foreign language students are not encouraged to use the Spanish, French, or German that they are learning inside the classroom outside the foreign language class. This view of language as a *subject* is detrimental to all language development. It encourages native-English-speaking students to disconnect their use of language in the hallways from their learning of French, or English grammar, or world literature in class. And it causes ELLs to feel that their bilingualism is not valued. Native English speakers are lauded for their baby steps in German or French, but ELLs typically do not receive the same accolades for their impressive bilingual skills.

In addition to valuing language, a school should embrace the multiple cultures within its walls. Many schools do in fact create positive opportunities for learning about food, dress, dance, and other visible cultural differences. Some schools also strive to build a global culture through maps and photos on walls, and diverse languages on bulletin boards. These are very positive steps! However, these steps only address the very obvious parts of culture.

To gain a more in-depth understanding of culture, we can envision culture as a flowering plant (see the Flower Model of Culture, Figure 1). In this model, the most obvious parts of culture are symbolized by the flower. Food, music, and dress are parts of culture that are easy to see and appreciate. Other customs and practices, represented by the leaves in the model, are also visible, but are more subtle. These may include behaviors such as body language, timeliness, and a child not looking an adult in the eyes. Finally, the roots represent invisible parts of culture, such as values, beliefs, and history. This model also shows that the roots are the least susceptible to change, while the flower is the most susceptible. As individuals acculturate to a new environment, their language, dress, food, and other obvious parts of culture may change most quickly as they seek to fit in, and their underlying values and beliefs may not change, or may change more slowly.

FIGURE 1. The Flower Model of Culture

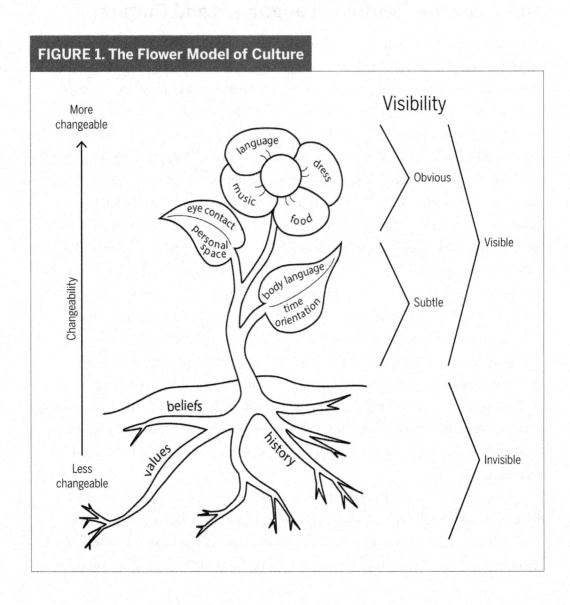

In a school environment, it may be easy to appreciate the obvious parts of culture, but more difficult to accept and understand subtle culture-driven behaviors such as standing just a little too close when conversing, failing to state opinions, or copying others' writing for an essay. Though we can certainly expect ELLs to eventually adapt to local norms, it is important to understand and accept the diverse ways in which people around the world interact and learn, with our first response always being, "I wonder if this behavior reflects culture?" rather than the gut reaction that the student is not trying to adapt, or worse—actively defying a school value or rule.

How can a school intentionally welcome multiple languages and cultures, and the students who bring them, within its walls? The following list can help to create a rich, global, welcoming environment:

1. **Provide basic professional development for all teachers on language and culture.** Teachers need to understand concepts such as surface and deep culture, and to create a "culture lens" through which ELL behaviors are viewed. Teachers also need to understand some basic concepts about language, such as the fact that bilingualism is an advantage (and that ELLs are emerging bilinguals), and the understanding that if students develop their first language, it will increase their ability to develop their second language. (See more in Chapter 4 on the positive impact of first language learning on second language learning.)

2. **Get rid of "English only" policies.** Most teachers who insist that ELLs spend a 6- or 8-hour school day all in a language that they are learning, without any breaks, have likely never tried to do this. Learning a language is mentally and physically exhausting. Students need breaks during which time they can "be themselves" and use their first language, in reading, writing, speaking, and listening. Students may also sometimes need to use their first language in class, to scaffold their learning. They may have legitimate questions about words or content, and the most efficient way they know to have their questions answered is to ask a friend who speaks the same language. There are, of course, times when students use their first language inappropriately—and this does not just apply to the ELLs. Native English speakers occasionally use their first language inappropriately, as well. Make sure any bans on talking apply to everyone in the room, and not just to those who happen to be speaking in Spanish or Korean.

3. **Foster multilingualism.** Along with not demanding "English only" should come active cultivation of other languages. Encourage everyone in the school to learn greetings in all the languages represented in the school, and to use them in the hallways. Post information in multiple languages. Get the foreign language

teachers on board with encouraging the use of languages being learned outside of the classroom. For example, native-English-speaking students could be encouraged to use the foreign languages they are learning for simple exchanges such as "Excuse me" and "What time is it?," outside the foreign language classroom. Assure teachers that having a multilingual school environment will *not* reduce the ELLs' learning of English. Rather, the increased climate of acceptance is likely to lower stress, increase participation, and increase English language acquisition.

If possible, create a multilingual section in your school media center. Allow for books and audio/visual media in other languages to be used at appropriate times. The internet can provide a multitude of language resources so that ELLs can both take a much-needed break from English learning and continue to develop their first language, and foreign language learners can further their language skills on topics of interest to them.

Ensuring that All Teachers are Trained, Skilled, and Empowered

Second language acquisition is a developmental process that is not specifically addressed in many teacher education programs. Some states in the United States require that all teachers take a course on meeting the needs of ELLs, but others do not (Samson & Collins, 2012). Even when teachers have had a course on meeting the needs of ELLs, there has not been clear consensus on what content should be covered in such a course (Samson & Collins, 2012). Some may focus mainly on the acculturation of the ELL to the local environment and providing accommodations in content classes while language is being learned. Some may not help teachers develop a strong understanding of how a person actually learns a new language.

General education teachers need a clear understanding of how to help ELLs acquire the English language needed to be successful in their math, science, or social studies classrooms. Some general education teachers may think teaching English is not a part of their job. However, they do actually teach English to all of their students, all the time. When presenting new content such as writing a geometry proof or constructing a lab report, they are indeed teaching students the English necessary to be successful in their class, and this English teaching can be extended to ELLs.

However, many teachers do not think of themselves as language teachers, and place the language needs of ELLs squarely on the shoulders of the TESOL professional— regardless of how much (or little) time this specialist has with each ELL. Along with actual

English language acquisition, TESOL professionals are often expected to ensure that ELLs somehow learn both the content and the accompanying academic language of any regular classes they are in—either by helping them as they "push in" to those classes or by working with them on content during "pull-out" times. (More information about push-in and pull-out models is provided in Chapter 6.) Content teachers sometimes do not understand how many new words and structures can be learned in a given time-frame, and how limited an ESOL teacher's time is with each student. Further, they may not be aware that the ESOL teacher often must divide what precious little ESOL instructional time he or she has among students of several different language levels.

Added to the need for increased understanding about the nature and reality of second language acquisition is the fact that, in many school systems, *all* teachers' roles and responsibilities are rapidly changing. In the United States, the recent introduction of the CCSS has prompted much discussion about how ELLs will meet the standards, and who bears the responsibility for ensuring that they do. (See, for example, Valdés, Kibler, & Walqui, 2014, and TESOL International Association's [TESOL's] professional paper, "Implementing the Common Core State Standards for ELs: The Changing Role of the ESL Teacher," 2013.) While the dust is far from settled on this discussion, no one disputes the fact that if ELLs are to achieve both high English proficiency and high academic standards, they must be actively learning language in all their classes—not just ESOL class. When this understanding is paired with the understanding that language is acquired through exposure to and use of language at the appropriate level—not through submersion in incomprehensible language, all teachers can begin to understand why it takes a school to develop an English speaker. It is not the solitary job of the ESOL teacher.

How can a school leader ensure that all teachers have the skills to address the needs of ELLs, and that ESOL teachers can have maximum effectiveness?

1. **Hire well-educated TESOL professionals.** As mentioned above, the role of the ESOL teacher in many schools is rapidly changing. A recent document published by TESOL states "ESL teachers must be redefined as experts, advocates, and consultants" and "the roles of principals and administrators also need to shift to support the CCSS and ESL teachers' new responsibilities" (TESOL, 2013, p. 9). With these changing roles, schools will be best served through the hiring of TESOL professionals, rather than simply ESOL teachers. All TESOL education programs are not created equally. (For a list of *minimal* qualifications for TESOL expertise, see the *Standards for the Recognition of Initial TESOL Programs in P–12 ESL Teacher Education*, TESOL, 2010.) Doing your homework before hiring will

eventually result in a lot less work, as you will have a TESOL professional capable of taking on leadership and training roles in the school. Take care when developing the appropriate job descriptions for the specific TESOL professional that your school needs. You have already started on this path by picking up this book.

2. **Empower your well-educated TESOL professional.** It is important to understand the ways in which the TESOL expert on staff is not like other specialists. Special educators, for example, are experts in characteristics of disabilities, specific pedagogy, and interventions that meet the needs of children with those learning characteristics. Simply not knowing the English language is not a disability, nor does it require intervention. The job of the TESOL professional on staff is to formulate individualized plans for placing each ELL in the best possible learning environment to gradually acquire the English language while continuing to learn content. And though ESOL is often viewed as a special class, like art or music, it is not an academic subject. Rather, it impacts students' learning in *all* subjects. So, knowing that the role of the TESOL professional is unlike that of other school specialists, consider well where this educator needs to have a voice and a role.

   For example, the TESOL professional should be empowered and administratively supported to provide training for general education teachers and staff. He or she will also need to ensure that parents of ELLs receive orientation and regular communication, which must often occur in languages other than English. It should go without saying that the TESOL professional needs time to actually teach English to ELLs. (How much time is needed for pull-out English language teaching depends on proficiency levels and other factors. See Chapter 6 for a discussion of where ELLs at various language levels may be best served in different grades.) Finally, the TESOL professional will likely be the one administering placement and progress tests, and documenting services and progress. These are time-consuming jobs and roles. Special attention must be given to assigning manageable caseloads. This means school administrators need to keep their finger on the pulse of their growing ELL population. Keeping count of the number of ELLs in your school will help you decide when it is time to hire additional TESOL professionals.

3. **Equip all teachers who teach ELLs with skills to further language acquisition in their classes.** All teachers should be prepared to address the unique language demands of the ELLs in their classroom. (This is not to say that all ELLs should *be* in all grade-level content classrooms. For more on placement of ELLs, see Chapter 6.) Content-area teachers have unique opportunities to help ELLs see how language works when talking about real ideas. For example, an ELL might learn in math about "if-then" sentences when a teacher poses a question such

as "If a car is traveling 60 miles per hour, (then) how long will it take to travel 100 miles?" and purposefully draws attention to "if" and the optional "then." Or, in social studies, a teacher might make the statement, "Justice Sonia Sotomayor has been on the U.S. Supreme Court since 2009." This could be followed by a moment of private conversation with an ELL, asking, "Does this sentence mean she is still in office? Or is she out of office now?" The teacher could point to the words *has been* and *since,* explaining that these words mean it is still happening. All this would take less than 30 seconds, as the rest of the class is engaged in another short reading or task.

Why do teachers not naturally have such language-focused conversations with ELLs? I would argue that there are four reasons: 1) They don't know enough about the English language, 2) they don't view it as their job, 3) they are teaching ELLs with very low English levels who really should not be in their classes, and 4) they simply don't think of it. All these factors can be addressed through intentional, focused professional development.

And who can provide this needed development? Your TESOL professional on staff. This educator is equipped to not only provide workshop or seminar-type training, but also to engage in rich collaboration with general educators. If your school day allows, provide time for content-area teachers to meet with TESOL professionals to learn more about second language acquisition, discuss the needs of certain students, and plan content-area lessons together. The TESOL professional may be able to provide appropriate scaffolds if he or she sees what the content-area teachers are teaching. In a picture-perfect scenario, encourage content-area teachers to visit ESOL pull-out sessions or, even better, invite the TESOL professional to team teach a lesson or two. As teachers interact more with each other, everyone will see an increase in ELLs' classroom participation and overall school success.

Creating School Schedules and Courses Conducive to Meeting ELL Needs

All the expertise and skill in the world will fail to result in an effective program for ELLs if the school schedule does not allow ELLs to be in the classes where they can best be served. Time and again, when I ask a teacher a question such as why the Level 1 ELLs are in social studies, a content area with high language demands and requiring considerable cultural background, I am told that it is because of scheduling. "Oh, the ESL teacher isn't available at that time" or "we can only pull them out during English class." School scheduling can indeed be a nightmare of a puzzle, and perhaps it is not possible to meet every learner's needs all the time. However, most educators would agree that it should still be our over-arching goal: to place ELLs where they can progress best in both language and content learning. What are some ways of thinking that can help to accomplish this goal?

1. **Prioritize the TESOL professional's time with ELLs when creating the school schedule.** TESOL professionals cannot effectively teach more than one language level or age group during the same time period, in the same classroom. The problem of a wide range of levels might be partially solved by investing in general education teachers and training them to address the needs of the intermediate and advanced level students, as proposed above. This would leave the TESOL professional free to work intensively with beginning ELLs (who are sometimes, but not always, newcomers with additional settlement and acculturation needs). However, intermediate-level students do also benefit from some pull-out time with a TESOL professional, and advanced students may benefit as well. So, it is crucial to determine who needs time with the TESOL professional, and to sched-ule in that time as the master schedule is being created. Including both TESOL professionals and classroom teachers in creating schedules for individual ELLs can ensure that the ELL's language needs are given prime consideration, while also taking care to place the student in content classes where he or she will be motivated and successful.

2. **Realize that ELLs at different levels will need to be in or out of different con-tent classes.** The issue of language level is such an important one that consider-able time is devoted to it in Chapter 6. In this first chapter, it will suffice to say that the lower the language proficiency level of the learner, and the higher the grade, the less likely it is that the learner will be well served in a regular classroom. This is especially true for more language-dense subjects like history and literature. Because learners at different proficiency levels have such vastly different needs, it is very important *not* to create a system in which all designated ELLs in one classroom are pulled out for instruction at the same time, into the same ESOL classroom, by the same TESOL professional. It is more important to have stu-dents of the same proficiency levels, taking into consideration age and grade level, in a given ESOL classroom. Personalized learning plans are the key to effective ELL placement.

3. **Ensure that intermediate and advanced ELLs continue their language learning through sheltered content classes, or time with teachers trained in language and content learning.** Just as harmful as putting a beginning ELL in a 10th-grade

history class is pulling an advanced ELL out of that class and placing him instead in an ESOL class. The advanced ELL does indeed need specialized language learning in that history class. However, it need not be the TESOL professional's job to provide it. Rather, there could be a sheltered course (an easier English version of the course) or sheltered instruction (a teacher providing easier English for an ELL, within the regular class) for the advanced-level ELL. (Sheltered instruction is addressed in more detail in Chapter 6.)

4. **Schedule teaching blocks of sufficient duration to make language learning feasible.** A final problem found in some schools, especially at the elementary level, is very short class times. A 20-minute block is simply not enough time to make progress in an ESOL class. By the time we account for movement to and from the ESOL classroom, and some light conversation as a warm-up, the length of instructional time may be down to 10 minutes. Teaching for language acquisition should be unhurried, organic, and stress free. It is hard to make a very short class period anything other than hurried, scripted, and probably stressful.

Conclusion

Well, how are you feeling? Are you convinced that a good understanding of English learning can transform your school? I hope you have been inspired to read on, given your influential role in your school. Where school leaders embrace language and cultural diversity, teachers and students are likely to do the same. Where school leaders place a high priority on skill and knowledge development to meet the needs of ELLs, teachers are likely to rise to the challenge, grateful that their leader has reasonable expectations and seeks to equip them to meet those expectations. And where school leaders consider the needs of ELLs when prioritizing and scheduling, the TESOL professional can effectively do his or her job, resulting in a well-functioning, effective program. It's a tall order, but not an impossible one. Remember, the TESOL professional is a resource you can call on to help answer some of the administrative quandaries you may have. As for the TESOL alphabet soup, he or she can help with those questions as well.

The remainder of this book will equip you with the foundational understanding needed to implement these ideas. And the pay-off is huge: teacher satisfaction, globally-minded students and staff, preparedness and confidence in the face of rising numbers of ELLs, and, of course, effectively meeting the language and content needs of ELLs.

GRAB AND GO!

Go to **www.tesol.org/school-leaders** to access the Grab and Go links and downloads for this chapter.

How Can a Good Understanding of English Learning Transform Your School?

1. Foster a school culture that values and welcomes multiple languages and cultures. See the **School Leaders' Professional Development Guide** in this book and online.

   - Provide training for all teachers on language and culture, and fostering multilingualism.

   - Get rid of "English only" policies.

2. Ensure that all teachers are appropriately trained and empowered. See the **School Leaders' Professional Development Guide** in this book and online.

   - Hire and empower well-educated TESOL professionals.

   - Equip all those who teach ELLs with skills to further language acquisition in their classes.

3. Create school schedules conducive to meeting ELL needs.

   - Acknowledge that ELLs at different levels will need to be in or out of different content classes. See **Table 3 in Chapter 6, Sample Placement Chart**.

   - Ensure that intermediate- and advanced-level ELLs continue their language learning through sheltered content classes, or with teachers trained in language and content learning.

   - Prioritize the TESOL professional's time when you create the school schedule.

   - Schedule teaching blocks of sufficient duration to make language learning feasible. See **Sample Schedule of an ESOL Specialist** online.

▦▦▦ References

Burchard, M. S., Dormer, J., & Fisler, J. (2015). *Interactions of self-efficacy, SLOs, teaching practices and student learning outcomes.* Manuscript in preparation.

National Center for Education Statistics, U.S. Department of Education. (2014). *The condition of education 2014* (NCES 2014–083). Retrieved from http://nces.ed.gov/fastfacts /display.asp?id=96

National Clearinghouse for English Language Acquisition. (2011, November). *The growing number of English learner students.* Retrieved from http://www.ncela.us/files/uploads /9/growingLEP_0809.pdf

Samson, J. F., & Collins, B. A. (2012). *Preparing all teachers to meet the needs of English language learners: Applying research to policy and practice for teacher effectiveness.* Washington, DC: Center for American Progress. Retrieved from http://files.eric.ed .gov/fulltext/ED535608.pdf

TESOL International Association. (2010). *Standards for the recognition of initial TESOL programs in P–12 ESL teacher education.* Alexandria, VA: Author. Retrieved from https://www.tesol.org/docs/books/the-revised-tesol-ncate-standards-for-the -recognition-of-initial-tesol-programs-in-p-12-esl-teacher-education-(2010-pdf). pdf?sfvrsn=2

TESOL International Association. (2013, April). *Implementing the Common Core State Standards for ELs: The changing role of the ESL teacher.* Alexandria, VA: Author. Retrieved from: http://www.tesol.org/docs/default-source/advocacy/ccss_convening _final-8-15-13.pdf?sfvrsn=8

Valdés, G., Kibler, A. & Walqui, A. (2014, March). Changes in the expertise of ESL professionals: Knowledge and action in an era of new standards. Alexandria, VA: TESOL International Association. Retrieved from http://www.tesol.org/docs/default -source/papers-and-briefs/professional-paper-26-march-2014.pdf?sfvrsn=2

Zong, J., & Batalova, J. (2015). The limited English proficient population in the United States. Retrieved from http://www.migrationpolicy.org/article/limited-english -proficient-population-united-states

CHAPTER 2

##

What Do You Need to Know About TESOL?

I n order to effectively meet the needs of English language learners (ELLs), all educators need to know a little about the unique world of teaching and learning English. Why is this world unique? How is the teaching and learning of English different from your average German or Spanish foreign language class? First, as a global language, the learning of English is often seen not as optional but as an essential life skill. It figures prominently in such issues as global migration, access to jobs, and opportunities for study. In addition, the dominance of English can result in conditions that are unfair and even harmful for those who do not speak it. In this chapter, we will learn about the global trend toward English, setting the stage for understanding what it means in today's world to take part in the expansion of the English language, whether by choice or not.

World Englishes

You are probably already familiar with the concept of dialects, and are aware that English has many, such as British English and American English, and further variations such as southern American English. Often, people distinguish such dialects through accents—differing features of the sounds of language. However, accent is not the only distinguishing feature of dialects. Geographic distance also results in the use of different words and expressions. For example, if you are reading a book that uses the term *apartment* rather than *flat* for a home within a building, you will probably conclude that the writer has learned a North American variety of English.

These dialects come from traditionally English-speaking countries. But there are other English dialects that may not as readily come to mind, for example, Indian English, and Singaporean English. Kachru (1985) illustrated the growing role of English in the world today through a series of concentric circles. He labeled the traditional English-speaking countries the *inner circle*, and the newer countries claiming English as a national or native language the *outer circle*. To these he adds the *expanding circle,* countries that do not have English as a national language but in which English plays a significant role as a language of international communication (see Figure 1). Kachru's view of World Englishes can give us a broader perspective as we consider the teaching and learning of English. There are many more users of English in the outer and expanding circles than there are in the inner circle, and this impacts the amount and type of English that students bring with them into our schools, as well as their future English needs.

The Native Speaker Problem

An understanding of World Englishes brings us to another problematic issue as we consider the English language: Who is a native English speaker, and does "nativeness" even belong in the conversation? A traditional definition of a native speaker might be a person who speaks his or her native language at home with all family members, in the local community, and in school with all teachers. However, many highly proficient, "native-like"

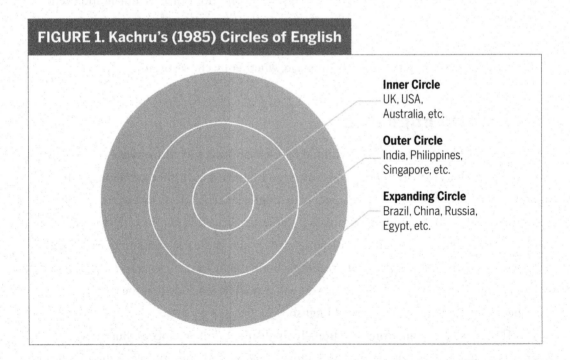

FIGURE 1. Kachru's (1985) Circles of English

Inner Circle
UK, USA, Australia, etc.

Outer Circle
India, Philippines, Singapore, etc.

Expanding Circle
Brazil, China, Russia, Egypt, etc.

English speakers do not fit that description. Today, many people speak a different first language at home but study in English, often acquiring a higher level of English than of their native language. Are these people native English speakers? A great deal of recent research has pointed to problems with a "native speaker standard," especially with regard to the common practice of preferring native speakers as English teachers (see Braine, 1999; Kamhi-Stein, 2004). We will address this problem in more depth later in this chapter, as we look at potential harms associated with the teaching of English. Here, it is sufficient to understand that language teachers need both language proficiency and teaching skill. Teachers are individuals, and these individuals can be either native speakers or nonnative speakers. Both can possess the essential qualities for language teaching.

The Problem of Correctness

The issues surrounding World Englishes and the difficulty of defining native speaker culminate in these questions: Whose English is "standard"? What English is "correct"? To what extent should so-called nonstandard varieties of English be accepted? Countries that have attempted to police languages and keep them "pure" have fought a losing battle. Why? Because languages always change over time. For example, take a look at this sentence: "Every student should get their book from the teacher." Technically, the possessive pronoun *their* should be *his/her* because the subject is singular. However, "he/she" is unwieldy and many people don't like to use it. So, "their" is often substituted. Many modern grammar books no longer identify this sentence as unquestionably "incorrect." With such changes taking place within the English language in speech communities all over the world, it will become more and more difficult to define correctness for the English language.

■ ■ ■ The Alphabet Soup of Teaching English

ESL . . . ELL . . . TESOL. . . . We defined these terms in Chapter 1, and these are only a few of the many letters in the TESOL alphabet soup bowl. Why are there so many different acronyms about teaching English? The teaching of English is nothing if not diverse—in terms of where it is taught, who is doing the teaching, who the learners are, and what the learners need. As teachers find that one term doesn't describe a given context very precisely, a new term is created. Sometimes, terminology is adopted without knowing enough about what the term actually means. So, misapplication of TESOL terminology is common, compounding the confusion. In this next section you will learn some of the more prominent terms, and how these should ideally be used in school settings. See also the acronym chart in Appendix A.

We'll begin with two of the most common acronyms: ESL and EFL. The first means "English as a second language." This term has been around for a very long time, and refers to the learning of English within an English-speaking context. So, an immigrant learning English in the United States could be said to be learning ESL, because English is the majority language in the United States. EFL has often been contrasted with ESL; EFL means "English as a foreign language." In many places around the world, English is learned in school as a foreign language, and it is not used in daily life as it is in an English-speaking context. So, in the past, it was very common to identify English-learning contexts as either ESL or EFL.

But this distinction poses some problems—problems which have given rise to new acronyms. First, for many individuals learning English, it is not a second, but a third, fourth, or fifth language. Second, many contexts are increasingly multilingual, making it difficult to distinguish an English environment from a non-English one. In international schools around the world, for example, the language on campus may be English even though the language outside the school is not. These realities have resulted in replacement terms for ESL and EFL, such as EAL, "English as an additional language," and ENL, "English as a new language." ESOL, "English for speakers of other languages" is gaining in popularity as a more all-encompassing term than ESL or EFL, and is the term used throughout this text for the learning of English by individuals who are school-aged or above and who have therefore already acquired one or more native languages prior to their introduction to English.

Two more terms related to English learning and speaking have to do with the spread of English as a global language. EIL means "English as an international language." Though we don't see this term a lot yet, as English becomes more global and perhaps less linked to specific places and cultures, we may see greater efforts to teach English for international communication. We already see this need in places where we see the use of "English as a lingua franca," or ELF. In such places, English is the medium of communication between individuals who have different native languages, but who both know some English.

Probably one of the most important learner-related terms used in school contexts is ELL, meaning "English language learner." It has sometimes been shortened to EL, or simply "English learner." In some schools, it is the term most often reached for when people are talking about the teaching of English as a second language, and is sometimes used as a subject of instruction, as in "I teach ELL" or "ELL is a big need in our school." In these uses, schools may be defining the term as "English language learning." It is most common, however, for "ELL" to refer to the English language *learner.*

When we begin to talk about the *teaching* of English, a whole new bowlful of acronyms is created. Thus, TESL is "teaching English as a second language," TEFL is "teaching English as a foreign language," and TESOL is "teaching English to speakers of other languages." (TESOL also refers to the international English language teachers' association.) In many parts of the world, ELT is a simple and widely used acronym meaning "English language teaching."

As the teaching of English has become professionalized, specialties have developed. We now have EAP, "English for academic purposes"—helping ELLs acquire academic language prior to or alongside their study in an English-medium context. Similarly, we have ESP, "English for specific purposes." This can refer to any type of study that has specialized language. Some examples are "business English," "English for tourism," and "medical English."

English teaching has also evolved in its methodologies. Several approaches or methods have become so prominent as to be recognized widely in the TESOL world. Among these are CALL, which refers to "Computer-assisted language learning," and TBLT, or "task-based language teaching." A pair of terms that is especially significant for school educators is CLIL, "content and language integrated learning," and CBI, "content-based instruction." These terms reflect the learning of English through other subject matter, such as math or science, which is the principle way in which the English language is acquired in K–12 schools, and which will be discussed more in Chapter 5.

There is one remaining, vast area in which acronyms abound: language tests, standards, benchmarks, and proficiency descriptors. These pose a problem for those in the field of English teaching first because they are so abundant, and second because they are so regional. An acronym that is important for daily use in one instructional context may be virtually unknown by professionals in another. Therefore, in this category I will simply introduce two terms that are fairly widely known. The first is WIDA, or "World Class Instructional Design for Assessment." WIDA has become widely used as a leveling, placement, and assessment system in English-medium schools around the world. The other acronym is for a test: the "Test of English as a Foreign Language," or TOEFL, as it is usually called. This test is widely used to document language proficiency for entrance into North American higher education institutions. The "TOEFL Junior" has also recently been developed, providing English proficiency scores for middle and high school students. Testing and assessment are discussed further in Chapter 6.

By now, you have probably had your fill of soup for one sitting! It is not necessary to remember and use all of these terms regularly, but there are a few which, when used correctly, can add clarity to conversations about the teaching of English in your school. A list of these, with simplified definitions and explanations, is provided at right.

▪▪▪ Potential Harms in TESOL

We want our work as educators to benefit students, not harm them. And in our English-medium schools, certainly students must learn English, and that learning is beneficial to them in our schools and beyond. However, a look at English learning worldwide, and even in our own communities, will reveal that the expansion of English may not be an unequivocal good in the world today. We do well to understand how the boon in English may pose threats to our societies, cultures, families, and even our educational systems.

Societal Harm

English learning has, in many places around the world, increased the social divide between the "haves" and "have nots" (Phillipson, 1992). Those who can speak English have good work and study opportunities. Those who cannot, sometimes do not. So the first societal harm is that the increasing requirement of English proficiency for all kinds of jobs, from hotel worker to secretary to business executive, may keep otherwise qualified individuals out of desired professions. In many places, English-learning programs or classes are woefully ineffective, as the TESOL profession suffers from a very high percentage of teachers with minimal or no training. Thus, more and more, English-learning

Useful Acronyms

TESOL: Teaching English to speakers of other languages. This is the most comprehensive term to depict the field of teaching English.

> *Examples*: "I want to hire a teacher who is trained in TESOL." "Our teachers need some professional development in TESOL."

ESOL: English for speakers of other languages. This is a good, comprehensive term for the English that students are learning. It is slightly better than "ESL," because for many learners English is not their second language.

> *Examples*: "We need to have separate ESOL classes for lower and higher level learners." "Higher level English learners don't need as many ESOL periods as lower level learners."

ELL: English language learner. Use this term for the students who are learning English as an additional language.

> *Examples*: "Our beginning ELLs need a lot of pull-out time with the ESOL teacher." "An advanced level ELL needs content teachers who are capable of furthering his or her language learning."

EAP: English for academic purposes. This is a good alternative to "ESOL" for higher level ELLs.

> *Examples*: "After ELLs have learned social English and graduated from ESOL classes, they will still take some EAP classes until they achieve advanced proficiency." "Our EAP classes help our ELLs to acquire the academic language that they need to succeed in school."

TESOL Professional: Someone who is well-trained in TESOL, and is capable of both teaching ESOL and training teachers in meeting the needs of ELLs.

ESOL Teacher: Someone who holds the position of "ESOL/ESL Teacher" within a school system. Ideally, this person would be a TESOL professional.

success is experienced by the rich few who can afford international study. More and more parents in other countries are finding ways to enroll their children in schools outside their home countries for the very purpose of learning English. We used to see international students going abroad mostly for college, but the trend now is to send high school, middle school, and even elementary students abroad, for an education in the coveted language of English. So, the jobs and opportunities often go to those who can afford international, or at least private school, study.

A second societal harm involves the preferential treatment of native-English-speaking teachers in the TESOL job market, due to the widespread myths that "if you can speak English you can teach it," and that it is preferable to learn a language from a native speaker. Thousands of English schools around the world seek to attract native speakers as teachers, providing well-paying jobs for adventure tourists whose only qualification is that they were born in an English-speaking country. The sad fact is that well-trained nonnative-English-speaking teachers in many places are not considered for English teaching jobs simply because English is not their first language. In reality, the ability to speak English, or "communicative competence," is only one of the skills needed by English teachers, and it is a skill that requires comprehensibility—not a native-like accent. Good English teachers also have a great deal of knowledge about how the English language works, understand the process of language acquisition, and know what teaching methods help learners acquire English. Nonnative English speakers may have an advantage in some of these areas, as they were once ELLs themselves.

Cultural and Familial Harm

The first harm in this section is the devastating loss of heritage languages among immigrants. Though research clearly shows that children fare better in second language acquisition if their first language is maintained and developed (Cummins, 2000), parents are still urged by uninformed teachers and well-intentioned others to speak English with their children at home. Home languages are often not sufficiently valued in schools. One interesting piece of evidence for this is that monolingual-English-speaking children who do succeed in acquiring a foreign language in high school or college are lauded for being "bilingual," while immigrant children with superior bilingual skills are often not praised for their bilingualism, but rather continue to be labeled as ELLs.

An additional harm among English-learning families is the distortion of healthy relationships within the family due to the emphasis on English. Parents who are under pressure to speak English with their children at home are in a bind. They do not have the English language skills to effectively parent their children through that language. They cannot teach, correct, support, or encourage in that language. Therefore, because they have been led to believe that English learning should be the top priority, they may concede their positions as fully functioning parents in the household. Parents may lose face and authority with their children due to their poor English language skills. Worse, the children are sometimes thrust into parental roles, as they become the family translators and spokespersons.

Educational Harm

The first way in which the spread of English is causing educational harm is, oddly enough, poor English learning. The need and clamor for English has far outpaced the supply of trained teachers and good curricula in some places. This is true even in some English-majority countries, where ELLs are still often taught by teachers with minimal or no training in TESOL. Even where ESOL teachers are trained, sometimes the training has been rushed and minimalized. To compound the problem, ESOL teachers' hands are often tied by entrenched and politicized educational systems. The losers are the students, who sometimes have very little to show for their years spent in ESOL classes. In the United States, an increasing problem is "long-term ELLs"—students who never acquire enough English to exit the ESOL program.

When students do not graduate from high school with college-ready English and also have not been able to develop their native language, their prospects for jobs and study become quite restricted. "Poor English learning can go hand in hand with lack of opportunity for students to develop strong academic skills in their home language. This frequently occurs in contexts where English becomes the major medium of communication and literacy in students' home languages is not promoted within the school" (Cummins, personal communication, July 2016).

Around the globe, one prominent contributor to a lack of linguistic college-readiness is the increasingly popular full English immersion schools. While immersion or bilingual education can be very effective for both language and content learning, as we will learn in Chapter 5, if not done well it puts students at a tremendous risk where higher education is concerned. According to De Mejía (2002), many such schools show poor results in both language and academic development. So, though immersion education can be a model for both language and content learning, it must be done well.

A final educational harm that bears mentioning concerns the education of undocumented children in the United States. In a landmark case in 1982, Plyler vs. Doe, the Supreme Court ruled that undocumented children could not be denied a public school education (See "Legal Issues for School Districts Related to the Education of Undocumented Children," National Education Association, 2009). A more recent U.S. Department of Education resource guide on supporting undocumented youth (2015) confirms that an educator's priority should be to educate and serve undocumented students just as they would any other students. Still, educators are sometimes uneasy when they become aware that a student is in the United States illegally. They may erroneously believe that they should report such a student, or they may struggle to find the emotional will to treat the student as they would any other student.

The resource guide on supporting undocumented youth (U.S. Department of Education, 2015) outlines well the vulnerability of this population:

> Undocumented students represent one of the most vulnerable groups served by U.S. schools. Estimates indicate that 80,000 undocumented youth turn 18 and approximately 65,000 graduate from high school every year. Just 54 percent of undocumented youth have at least a high school diploma, compared to 82 percent of their U.S.-born peers. Further, only 5 to 10 percent of undocumented high school graduates continue their education and enroll in an institution of higher education, and far fewer successfully graduate with a degree. (U.S. Department of Education, 2015, p. 3)

From The TESOL International Association "Position Statement Against Discrimination of Nonnative Speakers of English in the Field of TESOL" (2006)

TESOL strongly opposes discrimination against nonnative English speakers in the field of English language teaching. Rather, English language proficiency, teaching experience, and professionalism should be assessed along on a continuum of professional preparation. (Teachers of English to Speakers of Other Languages, 2006, p. 1)

> **From The TESOL International Association "Position Statement on English as a Global Language" (2008)**
>
> As a global professional association, TESOL values individual language rights, collaboration in a global community, and respect for diversity and multiculturalism. (Teachers of English to Speakers of Other Languages, 2008, p. 1)

Turning Harms Into Potential

While this litany of problems may seem discouraging, the intention here is to build a strong foundation of understanding about the impact of English learning around the world. We cannot be a part of the solution to these problems if we are not aware that they exist, and have some understanding of the forces that have contributed to these challenges.

The TESOL profession is leading the way to positive changes in all the areas of harm discussed above. For example, TESOL professionals and publications have taken a strong stand against the bias for native speakers as English teachers. TESOL International Association does not post job ads that include "native speaker" as a required qualification for an English teaching position, and attempts to inform and educate the public that *language proficiency* is needed, not *nativeness*. And TESOL professionals around the world are working to address underlying causes of the problem. For example, when working in Brazil, the private English schools in our area made an effort to educate the general public about the strengths of Brazilian English teachers. Over time, we saw a change in public opinion on this issue. And some organizations that in the past sent native English speakers to teach English in Indonesia are now, instead, helping local Indonesian English teachers to develop higher English proficiency so that they can teach effectively.

The TESOL profession also leads the way in promoting and embracing languages and cultures. We actively promote an additive view of language learning—that English should always be added to, but never replace, other languages. TESOL professionals believe that it is always valuable to learn the language or languages of one's students, especially if teaching in a setting where there is one dominant language (Snow, 2006). Some TESOL training programs require knowledge of more than one language in order to get a degree in

TESOL, believing that someone who has never attempted to learn an additional language is not ideally prepared to help learners who are engaged in this arduous task.

Educational harm is also frequently lessened by the work of active TESOL professionals around the world. TESOL as a field is a leader in methodological and learning innovation. Concepts such as authenticity, task-based and project-based learning, peer-work, learner autonomy, and self-assessment have broad applications for improving education beyond the English learning classroom. Often, as we teach English in places where teachers of other subjects may not have had access to training in modern pedagogy, there is a ripple effect of good classroom practice. Schools and communities benefit in many more ways than just increased proficiency in English.

■ ■ ■ Mitigating Harms: What You Can Do

Finally, *you* can lead the way in turning these potential challenges into opportunities on your school campus. How?

- You can ensure that the child who comes from a refugee camp with zero English has equal opportunity to become college-ready in your school as the child who has come from an elite international school.

- You can embrace a multicultural school climate, as was discussed in Chapter 1.

- You can help families maintain appropriate parent-child roles by taking care to provide official translators rather than relying on children for translation, and also by encouraging families to maintain the use of their native language at home.

- You can hire highly qualified TESOL professionals, and put in place systems that are likely to result in ELLs becoming highly proficient within a reasonable period of time.

■ ■ ■ Conclusion

This chapter may leave you feeling like a language learner who is learning TESOL-ese! It is a fairly young profession, with no shortage of challenges. However, speaking "TESOL" is no longer optional for school leaders in many places. The world has come knocking at our school doors. As we open those doors, it should be with a warm welcome into a space that can deliver language and academic success.

GRAB AND GO!

Go to **www.tesol.org/school-leaders** to access the
Grab and Go links and downloads for this chapter.

What Do You Need to Know About TESOL?

1. There are many legitimate varieties of English spoken all around the world. We should value these differences, and not hold ELLs to an artificial and uninformed "native speaker" standard.

   ■ Hire teachers and TESOL professionals who represent a variety of Englishes and who have a variety of accents.

   ■ Hire TESOL professionals who can act as resources on questions of dialect, correctness, and academic language standards.

2. There are many acronyms in TESOL, and they are helpful in understanding the world of English language learning and teaching. Use acronyms correctly to increase understanding.

   ■ Provide accurate labels on jobs and programs. See **Sample Job and Program Titles and Descriptions online**.

   ■ Use the short list of common acronyms in this chapter and the longer list in **Appendix A** of this book and online.

3. The global spread of English has sometimes caused some harm. Understand the potential for harm in your particular context, and work to turn possible harms into opportunities.

   ■ Ensure that children without previous exposure to English and/or with limited formal schooling can achieve full proficiency and college readiness in your school.

   ■ Value home languages and cultures, and encourage families to maintain and develop them.

   ■ Provide translation services for parents so that children are not acting as translators.

   ■ Hire a well-qualified TESOL professional who can train and support content teachers as they teach academic content to ELLs.

■ ■ ■ References

Braine, G. (Ed.). (1999). *Non-native educators in English language teaching.* Mahwah, NJ: Lawrence Erlbaum Associates.

Cummins, J. (1994). Semilingualism. In *Encyclopedia of language and linguistics* (2nd ed.). Oxford, United Kingdom: Elsevier Science Ltd.

Cummins, J. (2000). *Language, power, and pedagogy. Bilingual children in the crossfire.* Clevedon, England: Multilingual Matters.

De Mejía, A. (2002). *Power, prestige and bilingualism: International perspectives on elite bilingual education.* Clevedon, England: Multilingual Matters.

Kachru, B. B. (1985). Standards, codification and sociolinguistic realism: The English language in the outer circle. In R. Quirk & H. Widdowson (Eds.), *English in the world: Teaching and learning the language and literatures* (pp. 11–36). Cambridge, United Kingdom: Cambridge University Press.

Kamhi-Stein, L. (Ed.). (2004). *Learning and teaching from experience: Perspectives on non-native English-speaking professionals.* Ann Arbor, MI: University of Michigan Press.

National Education Association. (2009). Legal issues for school districts related to the education of undocumented children. Retrieved from http://www.nsba.org/sites /default/files/reports/Undocumented-Children.pdf

Phillipson, R. (1992). *Linguistic imperialism.* Oxford, United Kingdom: Oxford University Press.

Plyler v. Doe, 457 U.S. 202 (1982).

Snow, D. (2006). *More than a native speaker: An introduction to teaching English abroad.* Alexandria, VA: Teachers of English to Speakers of Other Languages, Inc.

Teachers of English to Speakers of Other Languages. (2006, March). Position statement against discrimination of nonnative speakers of English in the field of TESOL. Alexandria, VA: Author. Retrieved from https://www.tesol.org/docs/default-source /advocacy/position-statement-against-nnest-discrimination-march-2006.pdf?sfvrsn=2

Teachers of English to Speakers of Other Languages. (2008, March). Position statement on English as a global language. Alexandria, VA: Author. Retrieved from http://www.tesol .org/docs/pdf/10884.pdf?sfvrsn=2

U.S. Department of Education. (2015). Resource guide: Supporting undocumented youth. Retrieved from: http://www2.ed.gov/about/overview/focus/supporting-undocumented -youth.pdf

CHAPTER 3

::

What Does It Mean to "Know English"?

Without an appreciation for the myriad facets of language and its pervasiveness in all areas of life, it's difficult to grasp the monumental task faced by the English language learners (ELLs) in our schools. This chapter provides some foundational concepts about language, views of "correctness," the importance of language communities, and the inescapable links between language and culture. Throughout, it provides valuable information that is specific to the English language and which can help you understand why English is not a very easy language to learn.

▪▪▪ Language as a System and Language as Communication

Take a moment to come up with a definition of language. You may have come up with something like "words that we use to communicate." But we can quickly get into trouble with such a simple definition. How, for example, do we explain the completely different meanings of "take on" in the sentences "You shouldn't take on any more work" and "He has a good take on that problem"? Same words. Totally different meaning. And think of the phrase "You shouldn't have!" At face value this would be a negative reprimand. But most of us probably think of appreciation for a kind deed or gift being expressed through this phrase. If you have a hard time coming up with a more precise definition of language after considering these examples, you're in good company. Experts have spent years studying language, and defining and redefining it.

Though a single definition of language is unlikely to emerge, there are two common views of language: 1) language as a system and 2) language as communication. The first perspective views language primarily as a system of sounds, symbols, and structure. Grammar is part of this system, as are written symbols (such as the English alphabet) and the sounds of language, or its phonology. Language as a system tells us that the sentence "She black hair has" is not possible in English. It also tells us that "man" and "men," though very similar, are two different sound sets in English, with different meanings. Language as communication helps us understand that the sentence "Could you please close the door?" is actually a request in English, not a simple yes/no question, as it would appear to be solely based on the grammar. It also helps us explain the use of idioms and phrasal verbs. For example, the phrase "get out!" meaning "I can hardly believe it!" rather than "exit" can only be explained as we look at the various ways language is used by real groups of people, for real communication.

Ultimately, of course, we cannot separate language into two polar opposites called system and communication. Rather, these aspects of language are intertwined. In order to communicate any idea, we must call on our language system and use it as a tool to express our ideas. And even when language is taught as a system, the words and grammar that are used represent real ideas and communicate meanings. Still, these two different perspectives on language become significant in language teaching, because different methods or techniques usually favor one perspective over the other. For example, a traditional grammar class favors the systematic view of language, whereas a language class in which students are sitting in small groups telling others about their families favors communication.

Most language teachers today acknowledge that both views of language are important in the language learning classroom. We do want students to view language as a means of expressing ideas. We aim to enable learners to use language as a tool to communicate with others in verbal and written forms, often called communicative language teaching. However, the system of language provides the building blocks for achieving this communication. Without a shared system of grammar, sounds, and symbols, ideas cannot be communicated through language.

■ ■ ■ The Question of Correctness

How many times have you heard someone say about a perceived language error, "I know it's wrong, but everybody says it that way"? Take, for example, this utterance, perhaps overheard in a crowded coffee shop: "There's too many people in here. Let's go somewhere with less people." Those who pride themselves on grammatical correctness in English will notice two errors: 1) the use of the contracted form of *there is* rather than *there are*, resulting in lack of subject-verb agreement, and 2) the use of *less* rather than *fewer*, which shows a lack of understanding of the correct adjective to describe a countable plural noun. But many highly proficient English speakers would not notice these grammatical errors in normal, casual speech. So . . . are they indeed errors?

This question brings us to the topic of *descriptive* and *prescriptive* views of language. The prescriptive view is that there are prescribed grammar rules that should be followed regardless of how people use language. When many people "break" a given rule, as in the example above, this perspective sees the people as wrong and the rules as right. Prescriptivists put great stock in those who author grammar books, and similar authority figures, as being legitimate "keepers of the language." In some places, the prescriptivist view has been so strongly held that officials have regulated language use, determining, for example, what kinds of words and sentences were allowed to be on signs and public documents (e.g., Costa & Lambert, 2009).

However, history shows us that the prescriptivist view runs counter to the nature of language and the nature of the users of language—people. All languages change over time, and these changes come about by how people use the language. Words and structures may fall into disuse, or change in meaning. For example, words like "thou" and "thrice" were common in earlier forms of English, but are now virtually obsolete. Likewise, the pronoun "whom" is often now replaced by "who," and may eventually disappear. Words such as "bad," "gay," and "awful" have seen differing meanings and usages over time.

With a prescriptive view, the problem we run into is that, if the rules cannot change as the language changes, eventually they are out of sync with language that most people accept as clear, correct, and effective communication. Think for a moment about this sentence: "Which light do you want me to turn on?" Is it correct or not? If you say that it is incorrect, you probably feel this way because you were taught the rule "You can't end a sentence with a preposition." There's a problem, though: We often *do* end sentences with prepositions, and are hard pressed to find any suitable way to change a question like "Which light do you want me to turn on?" to *not* end in a preposition. So, what gives?

It is the prescriptive view of grammar that must give way to a descriptive view. In this view, language is seen as correct if the users of language see it as correct. You may be wondering how this works, given the fact that there are many users of language who may have different ideas about what is correct. The key is to understand the concept of language communities, and their importance in determining correctness. If presented with the sentence, "It ain't none of your business," we cannot just ask "Is this correct or incorrect?" We need additional information. Our next question must be "For whom?" (or who!), and in what context? Unless we know which language community we are talking about, we cannot determine correctness or incorrectness. Given the context of a movie set in the American Wild West, or a country song, we might call this language "correct." Given the context of an academic paper, we would not.

One of the common misconceptions about descriptivism and prescriptivism is that the latter has grammar rules and the former does not; nothing could be further from the truth. Language always has rules. If it did not, we could not use it for communication. Our understanding of the rules of language is critical in, for example, differentiating the meanings of the sentences "Jim gave Betty the book" and "Betty gave Jim the book." Only the word order changes in these sentences, and because we understand the rules of English grammar, we understand that in these sentences, the book ends up in different hands. The difference is not in the existence of rules, or the importance of rules. The difference lies in *how we arrive at the rules*. The prescriptive approach is to see grammar rules as coming from grammar books (or the grammarians who write them), and to believe that people should try to follow these prescribed rules. The descriptive approach believes that language communities are the keepers of their forms of language, and are the regulators of what is correct within their own language context.

So, an English teacher who takes a descriptive approach to language might view the statement "There's a lot of people here" in the context of informal coffee shop talk as perfectly correct. But this same sentence written in an academic paper might receive correction. The two language communities are different (coffee shop conversationalists vs. the community of academic English readers and writers), and thus the rules are different.

Form, Meaning, and Use

While the question of "correctness" is most often thought of in terms of the *form* of language, this is only one aspect of any utterance or text. To illustrate this, consider the sentence "I have 29 years." To proficient English speakers this sounds like a "wrong" way to give one's age in English. And an English teacher who has not given this much thought may hastily say that the student has made mistakes in English grammar. But, is there really a grammar mistake here? The word order is correct, there is subject-verb agreement, and the adjective is placed correctly before the noun. What is the error? In fact, there are no grammatical errors in this sentence. And yet still, it is *not* correct. Why? Because we don't state our age like that in English. We state it like this: "I am 29." Why? No particular reason. "I have 29 years" works well as a perfectly good age-stating template in many languages. But we just don't do it that way in English.

This element of language is called *use*. In addition to governing the forms that are correct, language communities determine what qualifies as correct usage. So, there really is justification sometimes for the simple explanation, "We just don't say it that way!"

In addition to form and use, all language has meaning. Sometimes the form, meaning, and use in a particular piece of language seem simple. Take, for instance, this sentence: "Debbie has a car." If we hear this sentence in isolation, it conveys very basic and straightforward information. But if we set this in the context of a discussion about how a group of college students will get to a conference that they all have to go to for a class, the impact of the sentence might change. While the form stays the same, the use of the sentence might be to suggest that Debbie could drive, and the meaning of the sentence might go even further to imply that Debbie is selfish and inconsiderate if she does not offer to drive. Language is rarely as straightforward in meaning and use and as its form may seem.

Language Communities

We have seen above how groups of people have the right to determine what is appropriate and correct language use within their communities, from the descriptivist perspective. Here we will look more at what some of these language communities are called, and how they relate to each other.

Most languages have different varieties, called dialects. These are differentiated through pronunciation, word choice, and sometimes even grammar. Let's take Canadian English as an example. While Canadian Anglophones largely share Standard American English (sometimes called "North American English") with those living in the United States, Canadian English speakers do have some dialectal differences. One is variations on the pronunciation of the vowel "o" in words like "poor" and "sorry." Where word choice is concerned, we can think of the famously known interjection "eh" as a question tag, in a sentence like "It's a beautiful day, eh?" Finally, Canadian English speakers might say "He is in hospital," borrowing British grammar, whereas English speakers in the United States would typically say "He is in *the* hospital." These differences are quite minor, and it is often very difficult to tell from speech patterns whether a speaker of Standard American

English is from Canada or the United States. In contrast, within the United States, pronunciation varies significantly from the North to the South, with little question as to a speaker's origin.

These are largely regional dialects. If a person grows up in the southern part of the United States, he or she will speak a southern American dialect, and if he grows up in the north or west, his or her speech will be closer to Standard American English. But are all dialects bounded by geography? No. Some language communities have identifiers other than geographical location. For example, Indian English is shared by communities in India but also by large Indian communities in other countries. And African American Vernacular English (AAVE) is shared by many African American communities, regardless of their location within the United States. This brings us to another term: English as an additional language or dialect—EALD. This term acknowledges that children coming from different dialects, such as AAVE, may have just as much need for ELL services in school as those coming from another language. Though they speak an English dialect, it may be so different from the standard dialect used in education that it is perceived as almost a different language.

"Knowing" a Language

What does it mean to "know" a language? You might come up with answers such as "knowing lots of words" or "knowing grammar." And you would be essentially right. The two main ingredients in language are words and meaningful combinations of those words, which we call "grammar" or "structure." But how many words and how much structure must you know before you can be said to *know* a language? Do you know a language if you can order food in a restaurant using that language? Or must you be able to give a speech or write an essay in a language before you can claim that you truly know it? Do you know a language if you can speak and understand it? Or what if you can read and write it, but your speaking and listening skills are weak?

There is, of course, no simple definition of what it means to know a language. A 4-year-old may know only 2,000 words in his native language, and yet we would hear him chatter away and say that he "knows" this language. On the other hand, a businessperson may learn 4,000 words in a foreign language and yet still be unable to converse fluently with international business partners. We would likely say that this person does not know the language very well. Some people use the written forms of a language extremely well, but struggle with pronunciation, and are thus hindered in their oral communication.

Others are the opposite, chatting away with great ease in social contexts, but unable to read even a fairly simple newspaper article. So, any answer to this question must be linked to a context and specific language usage.

We should not confuse "knowing a language" in the sense of *using* it, as all native speakers of any language do, with "knowing a language" in the sense of *talking about* it. Relatively few native speakers know the grammar of their native language well enough to teach that grammar to someone learning the language. This is a skill set of its own, called metalinguistic competence, that is unrelated to the ability to use a language for communication.

For example, a person who correctly says "This is a good book" knows the grammar of that sentence, whether or not she knows that the sentence comprises subject, verb, article, adjective, and singular noun. He or she knows the grammar of that sentence whether or not he or she can tell you that English word order is usually subject-verb-object (SVO) and that an adjective almost always precedes a noun in English. In other words, he or she knows the grammar of English, even if she does not have the metalinguistic competence to talk about it.

On the other hand, we do frequently talk about "knowing grammar" when we mean having metalinguistic competence. When someone says, regarding his or her native language, "I don't know grammar"—a frequent occurrence among native speakers of many languages—the person is actually talking about metalinguistic competence. Native speakers use the structures correctly in their native language, but they often do not know how to explain those structures. They do "know grammar" in that they use the language correctly, but they do not "know grammar" in the sense of having metalinguistic competence.

▨▨▨ Knowing the *English* Language

While all languages share the characteristics of language addressed above, all languages have distinctive characteristics as well. In this section, we will discuss some of the aspects of English that require special consideration.

Dialects

Above, we discussed the concept of dialect. One aspect of English that is different from many, if not most, languages is that it not only has many, many dialects, but it also has a number of standard dialects—that is, dialects that are held up as standards in academics and in the media. When people "learn English," their goal is usually to learn one of these standard varieties of English. Some of these are Standard American English (SAE), Standard British English (sometimes accompanied by "Received Pronunciation," often referred to simply as "RP"), and Standard Australian English. People are often quick to focus in on the differences between these dialects. There are word differences such as "lift" vs. "elevator"; pronunciation differences such as the variance in "er" endings; and even some grammatical differences, such as the use of "the" by Americans in the sentence "She is in the hospital" and the absence of "the" in the British version of this sentence. But the differences are minor considering the vast majority of the words, structures, and even pronunciations that are the same or very similar. Still, when speaking of "knowing the English language" the question of which English dialect we are talking about is sometimes a relevant one.

Accent

Variations in pronunciation, or accent, are sometimes a part of established English dialects, such as AAVE, Southern American English, Australian English, or Indian English. There are also individual speech variations, as different people say things in slightly different ways, even when speaking within the same dialect. Those who have learned English as an additional language may also be thought to have an accent that identifies them as someone whose first language was not English. However, it is a misconception to view nonnative speaker accents as problematic. Because the very term "native speaker" is virtually impossible to define (Phillipson, 1992), we should embrace diversity in accent, and there is no need to limit the number of different accents that ELLs are exposed to. Language acquisition goals should be defined by communication success and academic English proficiency, not the attainment of a particular accent.

Large Vocabulary

English is often said to have a larger vocabulary than other languages. This claim is not technically justified, at least not without elaborate parameters defining what does and does not constitute a word (e.g., do we only count root words, or also all their derivatives?), how dialectal differences are accounted for, and a host of other sticky issues that must be addressed in the counting of words. Still, the vocabulary of the English language is very large, with some dictionaries listing up to 600,000 entries. How many of these is the average native or highly proficient English speaker likely to know? Some estimates place the vocabulary of an educated adult at around 50,000 recognizable words (Weisler & Milekic, 1999). Considering the fact that even ELLs rated as advanced may only actively use around 5,000 words, the vastness of the English vocabulary is daunting, and may explain why ELLs often view their number one priority as learning words.

Particular Areas of Difficulty

An internet search for difficult items for ELLs will yield many different lists. Some linguistic items are difficult for learners coming from one native language, but not for another. We all know that learners will have different pronunciation difficulties depending on their native language. For example, speakers of Chinese may have difficulty pronouncing initial /w/ sounds, Spanish speakers may struggle to differentiate between short and long vowels, and Japanese speakers may confuse /l/ and /r/. Language groups often struggle in different areas with syntax as well. A Russian speaker may substitute a gendered pronoun for the neutral English word *it,* and a German speaker may not use a continuous verb tense when one is required in English.

Though such differences can and should inform our teaching in particular contexts, there are some areas of English that seem to be almost universal in the difficulty they pose for ELLs. One of these is articles. The use of the tiny words *a/an* and *the* can throw even advanced English learners into despair. Though many languages have articles, the rules governing their usage vary tremendously. In Portuguese, for example, a definite article is common before a proper noun (e.g., "The John is coming today"), whereas in English it is not. And one important rule governing article usage is whether the noun is definite or indefinite, which is often very intuitive in English, and difficult to explain with precision. Yet another noun category affecting article usage is *countable* and *uncountable.* This may seem fairly straightforward until we try to explain why a word like "information" is uncountable in English, though it is countable in many other languages.

Another area of difficulty for most English learners is phrasal verbs: verb-preposition combinations such as "get over," "take up," "turn on," and "put up with." Though some other languages do have phrasal verbs, it is generally agreed that English has more of them and uses them more frequently than other languages. In many cases, we have perfectly good single-word substitutes for phrasal verbs, such as "discover" for "find out" and "postpone" for "put off." Sometimes, these single words are even cognates with a word in the learner's native language. "Discover" would be much easier for a Brazilian ELL to understand, for example, because the Portuguese word "descobrir" sounds and looks similar. But the fact is that phrasal verbs are more common in most English usage contexts than their single word counterparts, and thus learners of English must engage in the arduous task of figuring out the meaning of a word combination like "turn on," which has nothing to do with the meanings of either "turn" or "on." An additional complication of phrasal verbs is that some are separable and others are not. If a phrasal verb is separable, its object can be inserted between the verb and preposition. For example, you can "turn on the light" or "turn the light on." If a phrasal verb is inseparable, the two parts must stay together. For example, we can say "she got over the illness" but we cannot say "she got the illness over."

We could discuss many other areas of difficulty, such as the multiple uses of "have," the strange variations on the verb "to be," and the complexity of clause structures. But the few points addressed here should suffice for our purpose: to show the breadth and depth of understanding that may be involved in answering the simple question, "What does it mean to know English?"

■ ■ ■ Knowing *Academic* English

Knowing the English language is only the very beginning of an ELL's task in school. When a learner has achieved the language skills outlined above, he or she has acquired basic social language—that which a young child has acquired fairly effortlessly in her native language. Cummins (1979) has called this social language basic interpersonal communication skills, or BICS. This language is needed in school for social interaction in the cafeteria and on the playground—and in the classroom as well, when interacting with classmates and teachers. But the greater language task in school is the acquisition of what Cummins (1979) calls cognitive academic language proficiency, or CALP. This is the language of school—of textbooks, essays, and oral reports. It includes specialized language in different content areas, such as the word "theorem" in geometry or "elevation" in geography. But it also includes words and phrases that simply are not common in informal language use, such the words "thus" and "frequently," or complex sentence constructions such as, "Despite his many failures as he attempted to create an electric light bulb, Thomas Edison's persistence eventually paid off."

The development of academic English will be addressed further in Chapter 5, when we talk about what it means to learn English in school. At this point, an awareness of the difference between BICS and CALP, and the long road toward academic English even after social English has been acquired, is sufficient.

■ ■ ■ Language and Culture

A final important factor connected to knowing a language is culture. Kramsch (1998) states, "Language is the principal means whereby we conduct our social lives. When it is used in contexts of communication, it is bound up with culture in multiple and complex ways" (p. 3). To this point we have only discussed what it means to know the language itself. But this is only one part of our understanding of knowing a language. An ELL who experiences an awkward silence after asking an older woman her age or asking a neighbor how much he paid for his new car will quickly learn that language competence is not only about knowing the right words and grammar. It is also about when, where, and with whom to use them.

We communicate using language, but we do so within a culture, and often are not even aware of how much culture influences the words we say, how we say them, and how we interpret the words of others. Just think for a moment about greetings. When learning a foreign language, we may fairly quickly and easily learn expressions used for greetings. But that is not enough. We need to know what expressions we can use with whom, and under what circumstances. For example, are different greetings appropriate at a sports event than at a formal dinner? Does the age of the person we are talking to matter? Does our social status in relation to that person matter? How quickly are greetings concluded and the move made to the topic of conversation? In some cultures, this transition happens much more slowly than in others, and launching too quickly into the topic at hand can be seen as rude and insensitive. So, it is important that we know, and teach, the language-culture connection as we assist students in learning English.

Snow (2007) discusses culture as being composed of shared knowledge, shared views, and shared patterns. For example, a piece of shared knowledge in Brazilian culture is that Brazil has won five World Cup titles. A shared view is that coffee is always sweetened, and is not off limits to children. A shared pattern is personally greeting everyone in the room upon entering and exiting a social event.

How might this understanding of culture shed light on the task that ELLs face in our schools? Imagine that a high school teacher in the United States is teaching the American classic *To Kill a Mockingbird*, a novel by Harper Lee, about the racial tensions of the American south in the 1930s. Her students are advanced ELLs preparing to enter an American university, so she feels they have adequate language skills to handle this text. However, the teacher discovers that her students, who are all from Asia, struggle more than she expected them to, and have difficulty even getting the main ideas in the story. Could a lack of shared knowledge be the problem?

As another example, let's look at the issue of plagiarism—a battle that anyone working with ELLs has certainly fought. Many teachers believe that when a student copies text without using proper citation, the student is just being lazy and stealing someone else's work. However, some cultures hold a very different perspective on copying: that it honors both the initial author and the teacher, in providing something "better" for the teacher to read. So, shared views are very important in addressing plagiarism. Without the shared view of unattributed copying as stealing and the purpose of writing as learning (rather than to present a perfectly written text to the teacher), it is difficult to make headway in this persistent problem.

These two examples merely scratch the surface on the myriad ways in which culture impacts language learning, effective communication, and the learning of academic content through a new language. A good ESOL program will ensure that students are acquiring competence in an additional culture as well as an additional language, while also taking care to value and respect the cultural perspectives that ELLs bring with them.

Conclusion

Many people underestimate the tremendous amount of learning that must be done in order to communicate well within a new language and culture. In schools, we may also underestimate the gap between what content-area teachers currently know about the English language and what they need to know in order to facilitate the English development of ELLs. Hopefully, this chapter has served to highlight some of these learning needs, and also to build an understanding of language correctness as contextual. All languages and dialects are legitimate and correct within their language communities. In school, however, we are tasked with helping students to develop Social and Academic English—the language of the school community.

GRAB AND GO!

Go to **www.tesol.org/school-leaders** to access the Grab and Go links and downloads for this chapter.

What Does It Mean to "Know English"?

1. Language is a system, but its function is communication. Ensure that ELLs are receiving instruction that enables them to *communicate* in English.

   - Hire TESOL professionals who have been trained in communicative language teaching, and who can train content-area teachers in fostering communicative language skills.

   - Understand that true communicative language development often is hindered when TESOL professionals are given curricula to cover from the general education classroom.

2. Common perceptions of correctness are frequently based not on real language use, but on artificial, prescriptive, grammar rules. Ensure that ELLs experience a program that seeks to develop real language competence in reading, writing, speaking, and listening, rather than one which focuses on passive knowledge about grammar or spelling rules.

   - Hire TESOL professionals who have been trained in communicative language teaching.

   - Allow the TESOL professional to select the curricula for pull-out ESOL classes.

3. English has a large vocabulary, and poses some particular areas of difficulty for learners (e.g., phrasal verbs and articles). Ensure that all teachers understand some of these difficulties, and are prepared to help ELLs as they learn.

   - Hire TESOL professionals who can help all teachers understand the particularities of the English language, and work with them to identify links between their content areas and the development of English language skills.

   - Ensure that the TESOL professional has ample time with ELLs at low proficiency levels to develop foundational language (BICS).

4. In addition to acquiring social language (BICS), students must acquire academic language (CALP). Ensure that academic language is a developmental focus in all classrooms.

   - Hire TESOL professionals who can collaborate with content-area teachers to identify and teach academic language pertinent to their subjects. (Science, math, social studies, and Common Core State Standards resources are available online.)

   - Help all teachers to see themselves as agents of language development for all students.

5. Language is inextricably linked to culture. Help all teachers to become aware of cultural knowledge that ELLs may not have.

   - Provide professional development on the topic of language and culture.

References

Costa, J., & Lambert, P. (2009). France and language(s): Old policies and new challenges in education. Towards a renewed framework? *CIDREE Yearbook: Language policy and practice in Europe—emerging challenges and innovative responses* (pp. 15–26). Brussels: CIDREE/DVO. Retrieved from http://www.english.illinois.edu/-people-/faculty/debaron/584/584reading/costa%20lambert%20frenchlangpol.pdf

Cummins, J. (1979). Cognitive/academic language proficiency, linguistic interdependence, the optimum age question and some other matters. *Working Papers on Bilingualism, 19*, 121–129.

Kramsch, C. (1998). *Language and culture.* Oxford, United Kingdom: Oxford University Press.

Phillipson, R. (1992). *Linguistic imperialism.* Oxford, United Kingdom: Oxford University Press.

Snow, D. (2007) *From language learner to language teacher: An introduction to teaching English as a foreign language.* Alexandria, VA: Teachers of English to Speakers of Other Languages.

Weisler, S., & Milekic, S. P. (1999). *Theory of language.* Cambridge, MA: MIT Press.

CHAPTER 4

::

How Does Someone Learn English?

How do people learn languages? This question becomes a pressing one when we are faced with students who do not speak the language of instruction in our classrooms. We wonder, "How quickly can I expect this student to 'catch on' to what we're doing in class?," "What could I do to help him learn faster?," and the ultimate question, "What *is* going on in that brain as he tries to make sense of everything?" These are important questions, as it is our understanding of second language acquisition (SLA) that determines what approach we take to content and language teaching, what policies we advocate as being fair to ELLs, and what responsibilities we embrace in the effort to facilitate language acquisition. In this chapter, we will look at first language acquisition, then extend our understanding into second language acquisition, including debunking some popular myths. Finally, we will look at the unique situation of those learning two languages from birth: simultaneous bilingualism.

▨▨▨ First Language Acquisition

We will consider different perspectives on how first, or native, languages are learned. The division of language learning theories into these categories is drawn from Lightbown and Spada (2013) in *How Languages Are Learned*. We will return to some of these perspectives later when we address theories of learning additional languages.

The Behaviorist Perspective

Skinner (1957) explained first language acquisition as imitation and reinforcement. For example, a child would hear "Daddy," say "da-da," then receive a great deal of positive feedback prompting him to say "da-da" again and again. Clearly, imitation accounts for a lot of our initial language learning. Children do hear language and do imitate what they hear. Only this process can explain how a child connects specific and different meanings to the sounds in "cookie" and "mommy" and "go."

However, behaviorism cannot account for the creativity that humans bring to language use. Though a child might learn words and meanings through imitation, children produce many utterances that they would not likely have heard anyone say. These would include sentences with errors, such as "me want cookie," and novel sentences such as "Daddy is blue," perhaps spoken after Daddy has had a mishap with a painting project. A child would not have heard these utterances, so she does not produce them due to imitation.

Though we know that behaviorism is incomplete in its ability to explain first language acquisition, it does seem to account for a lot of sound-meaning learning, and may also explain some of the *automaticity*, the ability to recall and use certain words and structures without thinking about them, that characterizes language fluency. Phrases such as "What's your name?," "What's wrong?," "I want a . . . ," "I'm gonna . . . ," and endless other language chunks are probably learned to the point of automaticity through repeated hearing and usage.

The Innatist Perspective

Chomsky (1959) challenged Skinner's (1957) assertions with his development of universal grammar. Chomsky argued that human beings are programmed to develop language. This was the only explanation, he claimed, for the fact that people can create grammatically correct utterances that they have never heard before.

A concept that is related to the notion of universal grammar is the critical period hypothesis. This is the idea that there is a "critical age" beyond which the first language cannot be easily acquired. Often, this critical age is said to coincide with puberty. Lenneberg (1967) popularized the critical period hypothesis, relating it to the concept of brain neuroplasticity. The critical period hypothesis is a theory that seems difficult to prove or disprove, due to the fact that children who do not adequately develop their first language almost always have additional factors that must be taken into consideration, such as lack of human nurture and care, brain dysfunction, or illness.

The Interactionist/Developmental Perspective

Since the 1990s, psychology has become more central to language learning research, prompting theories in which cognitive development and interaction play key roles. Critics of Chomsky (1959) have argued that the universal grammar explanation is not necessary because all language learning can be accounted for by more general learning theories. In other words, how we learn language is how we learn anything.

A key concept that stems from this perspective is cognitive constructivism. As an outgrowth of Swiss psychologist Piaget's (1964) work in cognitive development in the mid-1900s, cognitive constructivism says that people mentally construct meanings that make sense to them, and this is how they learn. First language acquisition would be explained, then, by the simple fact that language use is part and parcel of living our lives and meeting our needs, and that the task of survival results in language acquisition.

Some researchers have focused more on the social conditions that promote language learning than on what actually happens in the brain. Vygotsky (1978), a leading developmental theorist in the past century, proposed that learning takes place when an individual interacts with an interlocutor who is a more knowledgeable peer or teacher within his or her zone of proximal development, which is the space just above the learner's current understanding.

Vygotsky's (1978) work has often been linked to social constructivism. Whereas cognitive constructivism focuses on the mental construction of understanding, social constructivism focuses on the collaborative construction of meaning, through social interaction. Vygotsky's (1978) theory of zone of proximal development was not limited to language acquisition. It attempted to explain development and learning in general. However, we know that children do learn their native language through interaction, and it is not difficult to conceive of this interaction as more than just providing a language model, but as being integral to language development. In fact, studies have shown that babies respond more and differently to sounds uttered by a real person than sounds heard via audio or video. While we may not yet have a full grasp of what this means for language acquisition, we can be certain that the human factor plays a significant role in some way.

Brain Research

The exciting new cutting edge in language acquisition studies is brain research. Using noninvasive approaches, researchers can now gather data about how babies process language. We now know, for example, that out of the 600 consonants and 200 vowels found in human languages, babies begin to show preferences for the 40 or so present in their native language well before their first birthday, and baby babbling shows signs of differentiation according to what language is heard, by 10 months of age (Kuhl, 2010). This may explain the reality that pronunciation is the one area of language in which younger learners definitely have an advantage.

The critical period hypothesis is receiving renewed attention as well in brain studies of early language learning. It is very likely that there are differing critical periods for the development of different parts of language. The window for sound recognition, for example, may close much earlier than the window for sound production.

Possibly, one of the most fascinating discoveries in recent brain-related language development research is the necessity of social interaction. In one study, infants displayed a much greater awareness of sound differences in a foreign language introduced at nine months when language was spoken by a loving care-giver as opposed to being present through video (Kuhl, 2010). And even if infants are exposed to a multitude of non-language sounds, it is the language sounds coming from a human in close proximity that they will attempt to imitate.

■ ■ ■ Additional Language Acquisition

How do people learn an additional language, after developing fundamental competence in their native language by around age 4 or 5? This is the question addressed by studies in SLA—second language acquisition. Before getting into our topic here, it is useful to unpack this term. The first key word here is "second." Though the theories that we will look at apply equally well to the acquisition of third, fourth, and more languages, the term "SLA" is still dominant in describing the learning of any additional language, and so this is the term used in this book. The second important word to address is "acquisition." The phrase "language learning" may be more familiar to you than "language acquisition." In some of the theories that we will discuss, however, these are two different processes. Acquisition is the term used concerning language learning that takes place through exposure to and usage of the language, and is sometimes linked to true communicative competence. Learning, on the other hand, may refer to knowing about a language—having information about its grammar, vocabulary, and pronunciation—but perhaps not being able to use it well for communicative purposes.

We will consider four different perspectives that expand on those introduced in regard to first language acquisition (Lightbown & Spada, 2013), this time applying them to additional/second language acquisition, or SLA.

The Behaviorist Perspective

SLA theorists quickly applied Skinner's (1957) ideas on behaviorism to the learning of additional languages, and this perspective had a significant influence on second language education during the middle part of the 20th century. The most well-known approach associated with behaviorism was audiolingualism, or the Audiolingual Method. This method focused heavily on drills and repetition. Language labs and the repetition and emphasis on pronunciation that they could provide flourished as drilling, repetition, and memorization became equated with language learning.

Though behaviorism has taken a back seat to newer theories of language learning, it does provide a good explanation for the development of automaticity in language learning—the ability to use language chunks automatically and without much thought. Without automaticity, we would have to think of every word and structure before we spoke, and the cognitive load would make it very difficult to communicate.

The Innatist Perspective

Chomsky's (1959) theory of universal grammar also led to SLA applications. Chomsky did not make direct claims concerning whether or not universal grammar played a role in second language learning, but many other researchers have. The critical period hypothesis, likewise, has been applied to the acquisition of additional languages with frequent but unsubstantiated assertions that it explains why adults have a harder time learning languages than children. There is little evidence for this commonly held notion. In fact, Hakuta, Bialystok and Wiley (2003) conducted a study designed to show a decline in language acquisition after puberty, but found no such decline. They concluded that the critical period hypothesis was *not* supported for SLA.

A well-known second language theorist associated with the innatist perspective is Krashen (1977, 1981). In his monitor model, Krashen (1977) outlines five hypotheses related to SLA:

1. **The acquisition–learning hypothesis:** We acquire language through exposure, but we learn language through study.

2. **The monitor hypothesis:** The acquired system initiates utterances, but the learned system monitors and edits them.

3. **The natural order hypothesis:** Language features are acquired in a predictable sequence, which is roughly the same for all language learners. (This concept has also been called the internal syllabus.)

4. **The input hypothesis:** Acquisition occurs when the learner is exposed to language that is comprehensible but a bit above the learner's current operational level. In other words, the learner needs to receive comprehensible input. From this hypothesis, we get Krashen's (1977) famous "i + 1" model, where *i* represents the learner's current level (which we can call the independent level) and +1 represents the step above that level.

5. **The affective filter hypothesis:** A person's general emotional state affects language learning, either facilitating or hindering it.

During the latter part of the 20th century, Krashen's ideas were instrumental in moving language learning from rules and drills to communicative methodologies (often known as communicative language teaching). Still widely followed today, communicative methods focus on learning language through real communication, rather than through isolated rules and drills.

The Cognitivist Perspective

Since the 1990s, the psychological components of SLA have been theorized and researched, with an emphasis on cognition. Critics of Chomsky (1959) and Krashen (1977) have argued that all language learning can be accounted for by more general learning theories.

In terms of SLA, some key insights have grown from the cognitivist perspective. The interaction hypothesis has taken the field beyond the theory of comprehensible input to an understanding that the interaction associated with the input may be what prompts language learning. Mere input could be achieved, for example, by listening to a recording of a dialogue taking place in a market between a buyer and a seller. But far more learning takes place if the learner is a participant in such a dialogue. Swain (1985) extended the input hypothesis by creating an output hypothesis. She argues that it is only as students attempt to formulate comprehensible output that they notice and revise their own language use.

Another key insight stemming from this area of research is the importance of noticing or awareness. For example, a student may not internalize the *-ed* word ending as the way we talk about the past until she begins to notice the *-ed* endings on verbs. Noticing alone does not result in learning, but it is seen as necessary for learning. The recognition that part of a teacher's role may be to help students notice or become aware of certain grammatical features has resulted in the development of a strategy known as focus on form. While students are focused primarily on the meaning of language, the teacher will also take advantage of teachable moments to draw students' attention to critical structures and forms that are used to communicate meaning.

Finally, cognitive constructivism has found a place in second language acquisition theory. Such an approach to language learning is evident if a teacher chooses inductive (examples to rules) rather than deductive (rules to examples) learning activities, believing that the most effective and long-term language learning takes place when learners actively construct their own understandings. For example, a teacher may opt to present students with a text using past tense and have them discover "-ed" as a past tense verb marker, rather than presenting students with the past tense "-ed" rule and then instructing them to find examples in a text.

The Sociocultural Perspective

Some researchers have focused more on the social conditions that promote language learning than on what actually happens in the brain. Vygotsky (1978) proposed that learning takes place when an individual interacts with an interlocutor who is a more knowledgeable peer or teacher within his or her zone of proximal development. Vygotsky's zone of proximal development is much like Krashen's (1977) notion of i + 1. However, the zone of proximal development focuses on the interaction, while i + 1 refers to the level of language input, be it through interaction or not.

One approach to teaching that has a foundation in the sociocultural perspective is social constructivism. Like cognitive constructivism, the emphasis is on constructing meaning rather than receiving knowledge. But social constructivism adds an interactional component, saying that meaning is constructed socially, in dialogue with others. (See Reyes & Vallone, 2008, for a more in-depth look at both forms of constructivism in English language teaching.)

With the proliferation of computer and other technological sources for language acquisition, some have predicted that real flesh-and-blood language teachers may no longer be needed in the future. Happily, research is building that confirms the importance of human interaction in language learning. Kuhl (2010) reports that even in the area of pronunciation, which has been relegated to independent work in language labs for decades, social conditions are favored.

Synthesizing the Theories

The theories and research presented above are not mutually exclusive. In fact, they all have some validity, and can explain different parts of the language acquisition puzzle. Behaviorism may explain our learning of the words and language chunks that we hear frequently. Clearly we do pick up language at least partially due to exposure to meaningful input, as the innatists would claim. Cognition no doubt plays a role when we stop to think about which verb tense to use, or where an adjective belongs in relation to a noun. And the fact that we learn language by using it socially, in communication with others, would rarely be questioned. In short, each of these theories has built on the others, and likely all are relevant in any comprehensive explanation of language acquisition.

Brain Research

The cutting edge in SLA is in the area of brain research. Researchers are not only investigating the first language acquisition of infants, but also the acquisition of additional languages by individuals of all ages. TESOL International Association hosted a webinar in 2013 entitled, "Implications and Applications of the Latest Brain Research for English Language Learners and Teachers." According to presenters Bailey and Pransky, brain research is confirming many of our theories. For example, brain studies are substantiating the following:

- It is language *use* that results in language acquisition—not discrete item learning. Students have to speak to develop speaking, write to develop writing, and so on.

- The affective filter is important. Emotional factors override intellectual input.

- Working memory is our most fragile memory system, and is limited in time and capacity to about seven new items at one time, such as a typical 40–60 minute class period.

- Long-term vocabulary learning only happens by using the words in context.

- Our working memory is smaller in our second language than in our first, and is most efficient when working with patterns. This is why it is so important to learn new words and structures in context.

- We can process a lot more information if we can "chunk" it. Some chunks of language should be rote learned to the point of automaticity. For example, it is helpful to learn "at night" and "in the morning" as memorized chunks.

- Attention is important in language acquisition. We don't learn passively, but actively. For children, attention span can be calculated as age plus or minus 2 minutes. In other words, a 10-year-old has an attention span of 8–12 minutes.

- Students often experience cognitive overload in language classes. Signs of overload include confusion, distraction, expressions of frustration, and failure to connect new information to old.

- Students can process more information if it is meaningful. Therefore, meaningful chunks of language may be more effectively assimilated than isolated words.

Myths About Language Acquisition

Language acquisition is a subject about which most people have opinions. After all, everyone has learned a language, many people have watched their own children learn their native language, and many have engaged in second language learning—whether successfully or not. So, language acquisition is unlike, say, law or nuclear physics or computer technology. If those topics come up, nonexperts concede to experts, recognizing their lack of knowledge. With language acquisition, it's different. Many people believe that they know more about language acquisition than they actually do, and hence there are many popularly held myths about how people learn languages. Though you may not believe all of these myths, especially now that you have done some reading on language acquisition, it will nevertheless benefit you to become familiar with the myths, and the theories and research that debunk them.

Myth #1

Children learn languages more easily and quickly than adults.

The very simplistic nature of this statement regarding language acquisition, an extremely complex endeavor, should alert us to the fact that it cannot be unequivocally true. While it is undeniable that young children often seem to "pick up" languages in ways that adults may not, we need to look more closely at where this perception comes from, and what it really means. Young children do have a distinct advantage where pronunciation is concerned. They can often more easily hear and copy foreign sounds, perhaps with little effort. However, pronunciation is only one, rather small, aspect of language. Archibald (2005) states, "It is much more difficult to predict knowledge or ability in any of the other areas of communicative competence (syntax, cohesion, sociolinguistics, etc.) based on age of acquisition" (p. 420). Because pronunciation is one of the first characteristics of language use that we notice, good pronunciation can result in the perception that language skills are higher than they actually are. And on the other hand, poor pronunciation can mask significant knowledge of words and structures in older individuals.

Imagine that a family emigrates to the United States from Thailand. The family includes a 34-year-old father who is a businessman with a university degree, and a 4-year-old boy. The father enrolls in a full-time program to learn English, while the boy is sent to a typical American preschool. After a year, the father has probably learned at least 3,000 English words and many structures. He can probably communicate well in the supermarket and with neighbors at a community gathering. However, his pronunciation may sometimes be difficult to understand, and his written language may still have many spelling and grammar errors, as he has come from a native language with a totally different writing system. The son, on the other hand, has probably picked up about 1,000 words over the course of the year, not a lot less than his native-English-speaking playmates know, and may have native-like pronunciation. Due to his age, he has no written language to learn. He chats easily with his preschool friends, and everyone says "He has picked up English so quickly!" In reality, the father has learned much more in 1 year than the son. He has learned three times as many words, not to mention the whole English alphabet and writing system. But when he talks with his peers, native-speaking, educated Americans, he only has perhaps one-tenth the vocabulary that they have, and is sometimes misunderstood due to his heavy accent. Many people would compare the father and the son and come to the conclusion that "children pick up languages much more easily than adults." But our closer inspection reveals that the adult has learned much more language than the child over the same time period.

Many studies have disproved a simple correlation between young age and facility in language acquisition. For example, Snow and Hoefnagel-Hohle (1982) conducted research with native English speakers of all ages who were learning Dutch as a second language. In their study, children 3–5 years old scored the lowest on language tests, in all categories. In other words, older children, teens, and adults all outperformed the youngest group of children. A significant additional discovery was that the 12–15-year-olds showed the fastest language acquisition in all skill areas. More recent studies have confirmed that the early teen years may be an exceptionally opportune time for additional language acquisition— possibly even superior to earlier years (Taylor, 2013).

There is not a simple correlation between age and language acquisition in any area other than pronunciation. Even where pronunciation is concerned, most adult learners can arrive at full intelligibility, often with a minimal accent, given good instruction and hard work. Languages can be learned at all ages. There is no evidence to suggest otherwise.

Myth #2

It takes 1–2 years to acquire the English language.

The misconception that young learners pick up languages effortlessly has resulted in their sometimes not receiving needed language acquisition services in our schools. After all, if it is true that young learners just pick up languages, why waste money on providing special language acquisition programs for them? This false assumption led to studies on immigrant children in school. Cummins (2000), a prominent researcher on childhood language acquisition through schooling, developed the notions of basic interpersonal communication skills (BICS) and cognitive academic language proficiency (CALP). According to Cummins, BICS, our social language, is acquired fairly quickly over the course of 1–2 years. CALP, on the other hand, takes much longer to acquire. Children may require 5–7 years to catch up with native-speaking peers, where academic language—the language of textbooks and teacher talk—is concerned.

Does this hold true for adults as well? Yes. Collier (1989) found that roughly 5–7 years were required for an adult to reach competency that included being able to engage in academic tasks such as taking a college course. The important thing for us to remember is that it takes a very long time to fully acquire an additional language. It is not a simple or quick task at any age.

Myth #3

The more time people spend in a second or foreign language context, the more quickly they learn the language.

This seems like a tenable statement: The more time you spend immersed in English, the faster you will learn English. Again, though, language acquisition is complex. To fully explore the issue, we must ask questions such as these:

1. What about brain fatigue? Is there a time limit on the brain's capacity to absorb new language, rendering language input beyond that time useless?

2. What role does the native language play in acquiring a new language? Is it possible that the native language is important, and thus limiting the native language in favor of the new language is counterproductive?

3. What about the emotional factor? If hearing the new language beyond a certain time frame increases stress, does this stress limit language acquisition? Is it possible that continued exposure to the new language beyond an ideal time limit may actually decrease motivation and increase frustration, halting language acquisition?

These are not easy questions to answer, in part at least because any answers we could find would be dependent on the context. But simply asking the questions can cause us to rethink the hypothesis that "more is always better."

What do we know? We do know that children learning English make greater gains in English in dual language programs than in other English programs (Collier & Thomas, 2004). In dual language schooling, typically, children with two different native languages are served, and they each acquire the other language through a curriculum that is half in each language. (Dual language education is explored further in Chapter 6.) Studies comparing dual language and other English programs have shown that when half of a child's school day is spent in his or her native language, he or she learns more of the new language (Cummins, 1981; Ramirez, Yuen, & Ramey, 1991). If it were true that "more is always better," we would expect children in English-only programs to make greater gains in English. Studies in bilingual education also point to the advantage of using the native language to acquire the new language. Much of what we know about language comes from our native language, and it is naïve to think that we don't, or worse that we shouldn't, use that knowledge to help us acquire additional languages. Those of us who have learned languages as adults can attest to the value of notebooks filled with words and translations, comparisons made between the grammars of our first and second languages, and even connecting idioms and expressions in the new language with those we are familiar with in our native language. We simply *do* use our native language to acquire additional languages—and that's a good thing.

We also are learning more from recent brain research about things like short-term memory limits. You may recall the "seven-item limit" cited in the webinar by Bailey and Pransky (2013). Such research should alert us to the very real potential for brain fatigue in language acquisition. Again, readers who have experienced language learning will confirm the reality of brain fatigue. We have felt the limits; we have experienced the delight of an effortless conversation in our native language after hours of struggling with a foreign language; we have probably all said, at some point, "I need a break." And we were right: We *did* need a break.

Finally, recent brain research is proving Krashen's (1977) affective filter hypothesis, as we also saw in the Bailey and Pransky (2013) webinar. Stress does indeed inhibit language acquisition. Though undoubtedly whether and when increased time in the new language becomes a negative factor is very individual and contextual, there is no doubt that it can have negative ramifications. Talk to language learners who have been thrust into new language contexts with no break, and you will hear from at least some of them stories of exhaustion, demotivation, low self-esteem, and frustration—not the feelings we hope will prevail in a good school.

There is, of course, a lower time threshold as well. There can certainly be too little input in a language for acquisition to take place. Unfortunately, this is a reality that is all too common in foreign language classrooms around the world, where students may only have a couple hours in the foreign language per week. If language acquisition, as opposed to learning, is the goal, most would say this is not enough. But this does not mean that more is always better. You *can* have too much of a good thing.

Myth #4

Children learning English will learn faster if parents speak in English at home.

This myth is related to myth #3. If one believes that more English is always better, then it follows that parents should speak English in the home, to speed up the language acquisition process. We have seen above that more is not necessarily better, thus removing one commonly voiced reason why families learning English should speak English at home. But there are others as well.

First, we have very solid evidence that children do better in every way by retaining and continuing to develop their native language (e.g., Cummins, 2000; Genesee, 2007). Continued first language development is always positive with regard to learning a new language for academic achievement. Second, whether or not parents should speak English at home with their children should depend at least somewhat on the parents' level of English. What if their English is poor? This affects both the language models that children will hear and the scope and types of conversations in which the family can engage. For example, families with limited English may not be able to discuss in English complex topics such as a bullying incident at school or a political situation in their home country.

This brings us to the final, and possibly most important, reason why the language of the home should be the parents' native language(s): Parents need to be parents. Parenting is the most important task parents engage in at home—not language teaching. They need to use the language or languages in which they can best fulfill their responsibilities as parents, helping children to develop and grow into healthy and well-adjusted adults. A language is just a language. People can acquire it at any age. Parenting has a time limit, and the precious years afforded to parents to teach and nurture their children should not be sidelined by inflated notions of the importance of learning English.

Of course, context is everything in the field of SLA. Perhaps the picture changes if children are acquiring English within a non-English speaking country, and the parents have a very good command of English. Perhaps in such a situation there is no threat of losing the native language, as it is the language widely used outside the home. Perhaps, as well, the parents speak English very well, and can thus both provide good language models and engage in their parenting tasks using English. In such a context, there may be no harm, and may even be good, in using English in the home.

Still, all parents would do well to think seriously about any decision not to use their native language(s) with their children, in the home. There must be compelling reasons for this not to be the best choice.

Myth #5

The more children are immersed in English in school, the faster they will learn English.

This myth, as well, relates to myth #3. Again, if one believes that more of the new language is always better, it follows that schooling all in the second language would be best. As we saw above, more is not always better. And where children are acquiring a new language in school, we have very strong evidence pointing to the value of academic instruction in the native language. Collier and Thomas (2004) conducted research on SLA in school, investigating the effectiveness of many different models. In their research, dual language models outperformed English-only models. The Collier and Thomas (2004) study showed that this type of program is "the only program for English learners that fully closes the gap; in contrast, remedial models only partially close the gap" (p. 1).

In this study, "remedial models" are full-English models. That is, children are always either in ESOL classes or submerged in English-medium classrooms—regardless of whether or not they understand what is going on in those classrooms. In the Collier and

Thomas (2004) study, and in others, the full English model results in learning English more slowly—not more quickly.

Myth #6

All people acquire languages in the same way.

You may read this myth and immediately think "Ah . . . here's one that I *didn't* believe." We have made great strides in education, in understanding learner differences. However, if we could glimpse inside language learning classrooms around the world, we might quickly come to the conclusion that many teachers teach as if everyone did learn in the same way. We might observe students all engaged in the same activities, and often what they are doing involves a talking teacher, silent students, and a textbook.

How do language learners differ? Some investigations into this question have led researchers (See Ligthbown & Spada, 2013) to propose ideal language learner qualities, such as the following:

- Tolerance of ambiguity: the ability not to fixate on unknown language, but to attempt to get the gist of something that is read or heard.

- Willingness to communicate: the effort to engage in communication even when lacking some of the words and structures that are needed.

- Search for patterns: looking at language as a puzzle, and seeing patterns and connections.

However, language learners do not necessarily exhibit all these qualities, and others similar to them, all the time. So, the first way in which language learners may differ from one another is in the degree to which they possess these "ideal" language learner characteristics.

Learners also differ, of course, in personality. It is often thought that personality characteristics such as extroversion enhance language learning potential. In reality, this is unproven. Extroverts certainly have some qualities that may aid their language learning, but they may also listen less than would be ideal for optimal language acquisition, and they may be inclined to develop fluency at the expense of accuracy. Still, introversion and extroversion, and other personality differences, undoubtedly do play a role in the types of classroom activities that are likely to be motivating and stimulating for learners.

Another line of thinking about learner differences has to do with multiple intelligences. Popularized by Gardner (1993), this is the idea that learners vary in eight different types of intelligence: linguistic, mathematic, visual/spatial, body/kinesthetic, naturalistic, musical, interpersonal, and intrapersonal. Multiple intelligences theory has been applied to language acquisition in various ways, from the emphasis on kinesthetic activities, to the inclusion of music, to support for relationship-building within the classroom.

Probably the most well-known theory of learning styles is the categorization of learners as visual, auditory, or kinesthetic. Sometimes called modalities, these ways of learning have filtered into popular thinking in many places, with people labeling themselves as one of these three learner types.

Finally, this discussion would not be complete without mentioning cultural influences on language learning. Do Japanese learners acquire language just as well as others, even though they may choose to speak less? Do Americans learning foreign languages benefit more from learner choice than other nationalities might? Do Brazilian English learners do best with highly collaborative and relational classroom activities? Researchers are engaged in many studies about the effect of cultural differences on language acquisition, and any English teacher working with a specific cultural group would be well-served by investigating what cultural influences have been found.

Learners are different in all sorts of ways, and if a class is small, it behooves the teacher to know his or her learners well and teach in ways that will be most motivating and effective for them. However, learner differences should not be a noose around the neck of teachers of large classes. If a teacher has many students, the point to remember is that variety is needed. Regardless of learning style, all learners need to read (visual) and write (kinesthetic) and engage in oral communication (auditory). All learners benefit from diverse activities.

Myth #7

Language students learn and remember what they are taught.

Our final myth is sobering, given the fact that we are teachers. We presume that students will learn and remember what we teach them. In reality, again, language acquisition is much more complex than that. Let's recall Krashen's (1977) monitor model—specifically the natural order hypothesis. This says that students acquire language in a predetermined order, regardless of teaching. To illustrate, let's say I decide to teach a group of beginners the past perfect verb tense. Though my methods and teaching skills may be superb, my students will not acquire this tense. They might be able to memorize rules for forming it, but they will not be able to use it, because this structure is not acquired at the beginning level. If in this hypothetical lesson I am speaking to the learners in English using the "be" verb in sentences such as "This is the rule" and "These are the rules," my students *may* acquire "is" and "are," even though that is not what I taught. Why did students not learn what I taught, but learn what I did not teach? Because they learned the language that they were ready to learn. They learned what came next in the natural order of language acquisition, or, as it has sometimes been called, the internal syllabus.

The second half of this myth speaks of how well students remember what they have learned. It is sometimes said that students need at least six contacts with a word, in meaningful communication, before they remember it. In my own language learning efforts, sometimes the number seems to be much higher than this! The point is, we simply do not usually remember words that we hear or read once. Or twice. Or three times. We need repeated contacts with a word, within a meaningful context, before it "sticks," and moves to long-term memory. The obvious lesson for teachers is that review and practice are probably even more important than initial teaching in the long journey toward language proficiency. A key point to remember in language learning or teaching is this: "Learn a little; use a lot."

Simultaneous Bilingualism

It is natural for children to learn more than one native language. In fact, it has been suggested that around the world and throughout history, this was more the norm than the exception. Simultaneous bilingualism is the term sometimes used to describe the acquisition of two first, or native, languages. This is contrasted with sequential bilingualism, in which an additional language is acquired after age 4 or 5—the point at which we often say that the first language has been acquired.

We know that bilingualism is positive. It has been linked to higher cognitive abilities and delayed onset of dementia in later years. And of course it provides increased opportunities in work and study. So, raising a child bilingually has no real downside. However, it is good to understand what really does constitute raising a child bilingually, and how to make the experience as positive as possible for all concerned.

Do Bilingual Children Experience Delays?

Bilingual infants and toddlers have a much more complex language acquisition task than do monolingual children. Therefore, it is not unusual for their language development to be "delayed" in comparison to monolingual children in either of the languages. Bilingual children in the early school years may seem to have smaller vocabularies than their monolingual counterparts as well. However, if words from both languages are counted, the vocabulary of bilinguals is usually higher. The important thing to remember is that any delays when compared to monolinguals are short-lived. In the long-run, usually at least by the late elementary grades, bilinguals catch up to and often surpass their monolingual peers in language development.

How Should the Languages Be Separated?

The context for simultaneous bilingualism is normally one in which a child regularly interacts with individuals in two different languages, usually from birth. Simultaneous bilingualism most often occurs when either each parent speaks a different native language, and uses this language consistently with the child, or when a caregiver such as a nanny, grandparent, or neighbor spends a considerable amount of time with the child, and interacts with the child using a language different than that of the parents. It is widely thought that the best way to "divide" the languages is for each individual to speak consistently in one language, and only that language. There are two legitimate reasons for such an approach: 1) This may be a way to ensure that the child receives roughly equivalent input in each language, and 2) if each caregiver is speaking in his or her native language, this ensures that the child is receiving quality language input. However, this is certainly not the only way to raise a child bilingually. If parents are both proficient in both languages, for example, they may each use both languages with the child. What is important, according to Genesee (2007), well-known author on the topic of childhood bilingualism, is that children receive "continuous, sustained, and enriched exposure to both languages" (p. 8).

How Much Input in a Language Is Necessary?

Bilingual children may be at risk of not developing full competence in one of their languages, if they do not receive sufficient input. Genesee (2007) explains it this way:

> It is clear that children learning two languages at the same time do not need as much exposure to each language as monolingual children get for their one.

However, there is a minimum level of exposure below which the development of that language can be delayed and incomplete. We do not have solid scientific evidence to tell us what that minimum amount of exposure is. Our best guess at this time is that bilingual children must be exposed to a language during at least 30% of their total language exposure if their acquisition of that language is to proceed normally. Less exposure than this could result in incomplete acquisition of that language. (p. 6)

Is "Code-Switching" a Problem?

When bilingual children speak, they may switch between languages—often called "code-switching." There are many perfectly good reasons for this. The child rarely knows all the same words in each language, and code-switching allows him or her to express his or her meaning more precisely. Sometimes, as well, switching between languages is intentional and purposeful, and is done for specific communicative and social reasons. Recently, this practice has become known as translanguaging, and is viewed positively, as an expression of linguistic skill, not deficit (see, e.g., Creese & Blackledge, 2010; García & Wei, 2013).

Still, parents are rightfully concerned that their child knows which words belong to which language, and that he or she will eventually be able to speak consistently in one language. For the most part, concerns about code-switching are unfounded. Genesee (2007) says, "As long as most people in the child's family and community use only one language at a time, the child will learn that this is the appropriate way to use their two languages" (p. 6). So, we should take note of this reminder that using "one language at a time" is helpful for developing bilinguals, but we need not ban code-switching or be overly concerned about long-term development.

Can Children Lose Their First Language?

There seems to be enough evidence from both anecdotal and research sources to suggest that yes, this can indeed happen. If a young child is suddenly immersed in a new language environment, as may happen at school, for example, or through international adoption, and the first language is not maintained at home, the quick language acquisition that appears to take place may actually be a language replacement rather than a language addition (Bialystok & Hakuta, 1994). For this reason, we should think twice about very early language immersion experiences, placing priority on additive, not subtractive bilingualism whenever possible.

▪▪▪ Conclusion

From theories, to credible research studies, and now to actually viewing the language learning brain through new technology, we are beginning to accumulate fairly solid evidence of how people acquire additional languages. We can say with a great deal of certainty that language is not acquired by just memorizing words and grammar. Language must be used through reading, writing, speaking and listening in order for acquisition to take place. We also know that computers will not replace English teachers any time soon, as the human factor does make a difference—good news for those of us who desire to motivate, inspire, and equip the English learners in our classrooms.

GRAB AND GO!

Go to **www.tesol.org/school-leaders** to access the
Grab and Go links and downloads for this chapter.

How Does Someone Learn English?

1. Language that is used for real communication is largely acquired through use, not learned passively as an academic subject. ELLs need the appropriate opportunities, conditions, and time to acquire English.

   - Ensure that ELLs are in classes where language that students hear and read is comprehensible. See **Table 3 in Chapter 6, Sample Placement Chart**.

   - Ensure that ELLs have ample opportunities to speak and write using language at their current level. This is often accomplished through appropriate use of pair/group work in content classes, coupled with pull-out ESOL instruction. See **Table 3 in Chapter 6, Sample Placement Chart**.

   - Ensure that ELLs are allowed the time needed to acquire a language: normally 1–2 years to develop social language, and 5–7 years to develop academic language. Ensure that tests accurately assess what they are intended to assess (language or content), and do not penalize ELLs for normal language development.

2. There are many popular myths about language learning. Foster a school climate in which all teachers and families have an accurate understanding of language acquisition.

   - Create systems so that all teachers have information on the ELLs in their classrooms, including their language levels and appropriate language expectations. See **Basic ELL Information Sheet** online.

   - Create a school culture valuing "quality over quantity" where the use of English is concerned. Teachers should not worry about the use of other languages, but should ensure that English language use is accurately targeting language development needs at the different proficiency levels.

   - Provide orientation for parents of ELLs on the importance of maintaining and developing the first language. See **Sample PowerPoint for ELL Parent Orientation** online.

3. Some children are simultaneous bilinguals, that is, they are acquiring two first languages. Foster an awareness among teachers that this is a long-term advantage, and that short-term language delays in either language, or differences in language usage, are not problematic.

   - Provide professional development for all on some characteristics of bilingualism.

   - Encourage bilingual TESOL professionals to maintain consistent usage of the language of instruction, at the ELL's proficiency level.

   - Allow students to use multiple languages (code-switching, or translanguaging) in appropriate ways and contexts. See **Ten Ways to Make your School Language and Culture Friendly** online.

■ ■ ■ References

Archibald, J. (2005). Second language acquisition. In W. O'Grady, J. Archibald, M. Aronoff, & J. Reseller (Eds.), *Contemporary linguistics: An introduction* (5th ed.). New York, NY: Bedford.

Bailey, F., & Pransky, K. (2013, September 30). Implications and applications of the latest brain research for English language learners and teachers [webinar]. Presented by TESOL International Association.

Bialystok, E., & Hakuta, K. (1994). *In other words: The science and psychology of second-language acquisition.* New York, NY: Basic.

Chomsky, N. (1959). Review of "verbal behavior" by B. F. Skinner. *Language, 35,* 26–58.

Collier, V. P. (1989). How long? A synthesis of research on academic achievement in a second language. *TESOL Quarterly, 23,* 509–31.

Collier, V. P., & Thomas, W. P. (2004). The astounding effectiveness of dual language education for all. *NABE Journal of Research and Practice, 2*(1). Retrieved from http://hillcrest.wacoisd.org/UserFiles/Servers/Server_345/File/Publications/ELL/Dual%20language%20survey.pdf

Creese, A., & Blackledge, A. (2010). Translanguaging in the bilingual classroom: A pedagogy for learning and teaching? *The Modern Language Journal, 94*(1), 103–115.

Cummins, J. (1981). The role of primary language development in promoting educational success for language minority students. In *Schooling and language minority students: A theoretical framework* (pp. 3–49). Los Angeles, CA: California State University, Evaluation, Dissemination and Assessment Center.

Cummins, J. (2000). Language, power, and pedagogy. Bilingual children in the crossfire. Clevedon, England: Multilingual Matters.

García, O., & Wei, L. (2013). *Translanguaging: Language, bilingualism and education.* Basingstoke, United Kingdom: Palgrave Macmillan.

Gardner, H. (1993). *Multiple intelligence: The theory of practice.* New York, NY: Basic Books.

Genesee, F. (2007). A short guide to raising children bilingually. *Multilingual Living Magazine.* Retrieved from http://www.psych.mcgill.ca/perpg/fac/genesee/A%20Short%20Guide%20to%20Raising%20Children%20Bilingually.pdf

Hakuta, K., Bialystok, E., & Wiley, E. (2003). Critical evidence: A test of the critical-period hypothesis for second-language acquisition. *Psychological Science, 14*(1), 31–38.

Krashen, S. (1977). Some issues relating to the monitor model. In H. D. Brown, C. A. Yorio, & R. H. Crymes (Eds.), *On TESOL '77* (pp. 144–158). Washington, DC: TESOL.

Krashen, S. (1981). *Second language acquisition and second language learning.* New York, NY: Pergamon.

Kuhl, P. K. (2010). Brain mechanisms in early language acquisition. *Neuron, 67*(5), 713–727.

Lenneberg, E. H. (1967). *Biological foundations of language.* New York, NY: Wiley.

Lightbown, P. M., & Spada, N. (2013). *How languages are learned.* Oxford, United Kingdom: Oxford University Press.

Piaget, J. (1964). Part I: Cognitive development in children: Piaget development and learning. *Journal of Research in Science Teaching, 2*(3), 176–186.

Ramirez, J. D., Yuen, S. D., & Ramey, D. R. (1991). Longitudinal study of structured English immersion strategy, early-exit and late-exit transitional bilingual education programs for language minority children. Final Report. Volumes 1 & 2. San Mateo, CA: Aguirre International.

Reyes, S. A., & Vallone, T. L. (2008). *Constructivist strategies for teaching English language learners.* Thousand Oaks, CA: Corwin Press.

Skinner, B. F. (1957). *Verbal behavior.* New York, NY: Appleton-Century-Crofts.

Snow, C., & Hoefnagel-Hohle, M. (1982). The critical period for language acquisition: evidence from second language learning. In S. Krashen, R. Scarcell, & M. Long (Eds.), *Issues in second language research* (pp. 93–113). London, England: Newbury House.

Swain, M. (1985). Communicative competence: Some roles of comprehensible input and comprehensible output in its development. In S. Gass & C. Madden (Eds.), *Input in second language acquisition* (pp. 235–253). Rowley, MA: Newbury House.

Taylor, F. (2013). *Self and identity in adolescent foreign language learning.* Bristol, United Kingdom: Multilingual Matters.

Vygotsky, L. S. (1978). *Mind in society.* Cambridge, MA: Harvard University Press.

CHAPTER 5

■■
■■

How Does Someone Learn English in School?

■■■ The Shift to Learning English Through Schooling

n the distant past, English classes were largely composed of grammar, reading, and translation (the "Grammar Translation Approach") or oral drills and memorized dialogues (the "Audiolingual Approach"). In the less distant past, English classrooms became spaces for experimenting with methodology, under a false belief that an ideal method existed, just waiting to be discovered. The eventual understanding that no such magic bullet exists for language acquisition has spawned a shift in thinking about language learning: a shift in emphasis from language teaching to language acquisition. This shift has brought us communicative language classrooms, where the goal is not to learn grammar or memorize vocabulary and dialogues in class, but to actively listen, speak, read, and write in the new language, for meaningful communication. Even more important, however, this shift in thinking has caused parents around the world to look to regular schooling as opposed to English classes as a means for their children to acquire English.

Even when parents have not actively sought out a K–12 (kindergarten through grade 12) learning environment for the main purpose of helping their child acquire English, as in the case of immigrants, parents still largely believe that the K–12 environment will serve that purpose. They believe that their children will "pick up" English as a result of engaging in schooling in English. Are these parents right? *Is* K–12 schooling a good way to learn a language? Yes, it is. However, it is neither automatic nor guaranteed, as evidenced by the much higher high school dropout rate among English language learners (ELLs): "Research repeatedly shows that EL students are about twice as likely to drop out as native and fluent English speakers" (Callahan, 2013). In fact, the mere existence of long-term ELLs in our schools, those who have not progressed out of ELL designation within 6 years, points to the ineffectiveness of English language acquisition in some K–12 schools (Olsen, 2014).

This chapter outlines the factors needed for success in K–12 English language learning. We begin by looking at what characterizes "effectiveness" in teachers, students, and methods. We then look at principles governing language acquisition, and how these play out in language classrooms. Finally, we look specifically at the integration of language and academic content, and various types of programs that serve these dual purposes.

■ ■ ■ Teacher Qualities

Before we dive in to the qualities required of English teachers, we need to address this question: Who is the English teacher? We saw in Chapter 1 the important role played by content-area teachers in the language development of ELLs. So, in response to this question, we might say that *English teachers are all those who facilitate the English language acquisition of an ELL.* The most successful school environments for ELLs are those in which all teachers, and even others who interact with the student, understand some principles of language acquisition, share in the goals of creating a welcoming and multicultural environment, and accept responsibility for playing a part, no matter how small, in the ELL's progress toward English proficiency. Therefore, as we discuss teachers, learners, and methods in this section, we are not only addressing ESOL teachers and ESOL classrooms. Rather, we will make connections to virtually every part of the school environment.

What knowledge and skills do teachers need in order to be able to facilitate language acquisition? Effective teachers possess two skill sets: 1) language skill, and 2) teaching skill, as shown in Figure 1 (Dormer, 2011).

The first requirement seems obvious to most: you can't teach a language if you can't speak it. This ability to speak or use a language we call communicative competence. We develop this ability naturally in our native language. Usually by the age of 5 or 6, we are fully proficient in basic communication skills. We can both meet our needs and build relationships with others by using language. Additionally, we are able to use language to think, entertain, and understand the world around us. Though a child of 5 or 6 can be said to be fully proficient in his or her native language, we saw in Chapter 3 the many complexities in using a language competently. This is why language development continues through to adulthood and beyond.

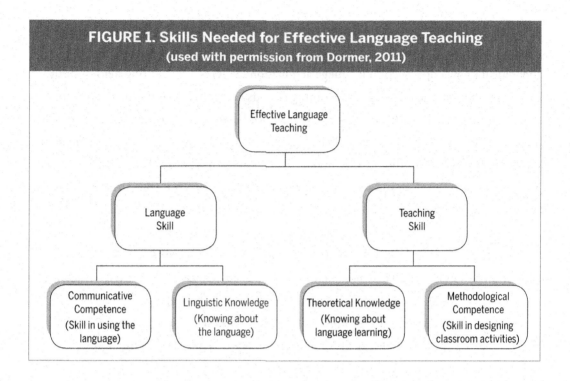

FIGURE 1. Skills Needed for Effective Language Teaching
(used with permission from Dormer, 2011)

Though we almost always develop full communicative competence in our native language, we do not automatically develop linguistic knowledge. This is knowing *about* language. Most of us can recall grammar lessons in school, where the goal was to develop our linguistic knowledge—an understanding of verbs, adjectives, adverbs, clause structures, and so on. Unfortunately, most of that did not "stick" for many of us, and even if it did, it usually did not result in a deep understanding of how our language is put together. For example, most native English speakers are hard pressed to answer simple questions like "How many verb tenses are there in English?" and "Why can we say 'turn on the light' but not 'turn on it'"?

Content teachers in the school may not need to know how many verb tenses there are in English. But they do need access to a TESOL professional on staff who can answer their questions about the English language as they integrate language development into their classes. And where language directly impacts content, teachers do need appropriate linguistic skill. For example, a history teacher should be able to explain why past perfect tense is used in the sentence "The Native American population had been high, but after colonization their numbers dwindled due to war and disease."

Teaching skill is the second requirement for effective language teaching. In language teacher education programs, the starting point for developing language teaching skill is theoretical knowledge. Second language acquisition (SLA) is a fascinating field of study. How does the brain make sense of incoming sounds and symbols and transform them into meaning? What conditions must be present for language acquisition, and why? When attempts at language learning fail, what has gone wrong? Our brief overview in Chapter 4 hopefully demonstrated that SLA is an ongoing, complex field of study. The TESOL professional in the school should be very well-versed in SLA. But even content-area teachers need some understanding of how the ELLs in their classrooms are learning language.

After laying a foundation of theoretical understanding in SLA, teachers can develop methodological competence: the ability to choose classroom activities and techniques that will result in language learning. Teachers need a storehouse of activities to teach the different language skills (speaking, listening, reading, and writing), different language proficiency levels, different age groups, and different class sizes. Teachers need the ability to select classroom tasks which will sometimes foster fluency and sometimes accuracy. Teachers need good methods to perk up a sleepy afternoon class or to keep an overactive group of third-graders from tearing up the classroom. In essence, teachers must know what to do in the classroom so that students can acquire the language. And content teachers must know how to integrate these all-important language acquisition techniques into the teaching of their content as well.

So . . . is a teacher who has language skill and teaching skill all set to foster English language development? Not quite! The most superb skill sets can become virtually meaningless without good teacher dispositions—the attitudes, beliefs, and values that teachers bring into and live out in their classrooms. We do not need research to tell us, for example, that cheerful, positive teachers are probably more effective than boring, pessimistic ones. Enthusiasm, concern and respect for students, and reflection on teaching are just a few of the teacher characteristics that we know have a huge impact on teaching effectiveness (See, e.g., Dormer, 2011, and Harmer, 2015). This is even truer where cross-cultural teaching is concerned. Teachers may be imperfect in their ability to select good methodologies or to integrate language and content learning, but if they create classroom spaces where diverse cultures are appreciated and the class as a whole seeks to help and encourage the ELL, a lot of good can result even in the midst of imperfect pedagogy.

At the end of the day, what is an English teacher? Fundamentally, teaching is all about the learner. Our working definition moving forward will be: *Teaching English is enabling someone to learn English.*

■ ■ ■ Principles of Language Acquisition

The definition above points us in the direction of the learner, and our ultimate goal of equipping the learner with the resources and skills to use the language. Unfortunately, many learners, like many teachers, do not understand language acquisition very well. In addition, many have experienced previous education that actively worked against effective language acquisition. So, it is necessary for teachers and school leaders to understand not only good language teaching, but also the principles of good language learning. It ultimately often falls on us to help our ELLs engage in the kinds of activities that result in language acquisition.

As we saw above, we have shifted away from a view of language teaching as methodology, in favor of a view that emphasizes principles of language acquisition. Brown (2007) developed a series of principles that have been very influential in language teaching. We will look at some of these principles, and how they might be applied in K–12 language acquisition.

1. Automaticity

Many components of language must be learned to the point of automaticity. When we use a language, we cannot consciously think about all the words and grammar that we are using. Some parts of language must be readily available in our subconscious, to be used automatically. When we read earlier about the behavioristic view of language acquisition, we noted that behaviorism probably does indeed account for the chunks of language that we know and can use automatically, without much thought. If asked "Where are you going?" we don't have to process the first part of our response at all. We automatically think "I'm . . ." or "to. . . ." These automatically-processed words and structures leave us with enough brain power to make conscious decisions about other words, such as recalling where we are going.

What is the implication of this principle for language teaching? Students do require practice! Using words and structures again and again is not time wasted. With language, simply knowing is not enough. It is in the using of language that the brain pathways are formed for automaticity. However, a problem we frequently see is that repetition in language classes is boring and meaningless. We now know that even repeated language use must be meaningful. Mantra-like chanting of words or phrases again and again is only minimally helpful. Real automaticity is developed through repeated *meaningful* language use. For example, imagine a task in which students fill out a survey about their classmates' favorite foods. A student might repeat the phrase "What is your favorite . . ." 20 times, but each time the phrase is meaningful, as the student learns about his or her classmates' preferences.

2. Meaningful Learning

We learned in Chapter 4 about the importance of meaningfulness in the language learning classroom. We know that meaningful learning results in more long-term retention than rote learning. Language learners need to understand the language that they are hearing and using, and the topics discussed should be of interest to them.

While I have yet to hear anyone disagree with this, it is amazing how often I see ELLs struggling to get something out of boring or incomprehensible classes. Whether it is an ESOL teacher who can't resist expounding on a punctuation rule or a content class in which the ELL comprehends virtually nothing, precious hours or minutes are wasted on content that is not meaningful.

How can teachers ensure meaningfulness for their learners? Here are some guidelines:

a. **Know your learners.** As we have seen, context is everything in language teaching. Cultures are different, learners are different, and learner goals are different. Any effort at creating a meaningful classroom must begin with the learners. We should choose topics and activities that are of interest to them, and which help them meet their goals.

b. **Focus on the people in the room.** One problem with traditional textbook-focused teaching is that it is impersonal. In an ESOL class it is inherently more meaningful to talk about the families of the people in the room (students and teacher) than a fictitious family in a course book, for example. Sometimes texts and curricula are mandated, and teachers feel that they have little latitude in selecting class content that really meets the needs of the learners. Sometimes, as well, teachers have the opportunity to create their own lessons, but insufficient training to do so. Inasmuch as possible, though, lessons need to be about the people in the room.

c. **Pay attention to language level.** Language level is everything in language acquisition. An otherwise meaningful activity can quickly become either boring or frustrating if the language required is either too easy or too difficult. For example, a student asked to survey classmates on their food preferences in an ESOL class may feel that time is being wasted if the language comes easily to him. On the other hand, a beginning ELL who is asked to participate in a group project comparing and contrasting the Union and Confederate armies in an American History classroom will likely find not only the language but also the content meaningless. The student needs a much stronger language and culture foundation before such a class experience could provide any real language or content learning.

3. Intrinsic Motivation

Intrinsic motivation is that which comes from personal desire, and which will remain steady through the trials and frustrations of language acquisition. A learner who only has extrinsic, or external motivation will often give up during the long haul of learning a language.

Some language learners already have intrinsic motivation when they step into our classrooms. We can see it from their "tell me more" attitudes and their drive to practice and use new language. But other students may not have such strong internal motivation. When this is the case, how can teachers foster intrinsic motivation in language learners? The answer to this question depends a great deal on the context—the age of the learners, their language level, and their goals. But some general guidelines include the following:

a. **Ensure and highlight success.** Some learners have experienced little success in school. Others have experienced success without knowing it. Perhaps they did learn, but performed poorly on tests and did not achieve good grades. If only grades are rewarded, a student can be unaware of his successes in language or content learning. When we make our classrooms spaces in which true learning is recognized and rewarded, students begin to feel pride in their learning accomplishments, and this leads to intrinsic motivation.

b. **Make the classroom time inviting.** Learners who do not arrive with built-in motivation may be that way precisely because they have difficulty focusing on a long-term goal. So, simply reminding them that they need English for their future may not help. However, making the current physical classroom space and time inviting and appealing may help them invest at least during the class period, and this can eventually plant seeds of intrinsic motivation.

c. **Plan for diminishing external motivators.** Sometimes external motivators such as food, points, a reduction in homework, and so on can be useful to kick-start motivation. However, use of external motivators can backfire as well. I once saw a delightful class of first graders learning "greater than" and "less than." They were eagerly showing their mastery of both the mathematical concepts and the language structure through a fun and well-designed activity. Then, the teacher said, "Okay, now we'll do it for points!" Immediately the children's focus shifted from the math and the language to the competition between teams. Complaints about fairness ensued. No more language or math was learned during that period, and the satisfaction that the children had been experiencing in learning was gone.

d. **Build learner autonomy.** Teach students how to take responsibility for their own learning. This may begin by providing students with limited choices over learning activities. As students become more accustomed to directing their own learning, this may include more substantial decisions over targeted learning goals, and may include self-assessment of the realization of those goals. As students take more responsibility for their English learning, intrinsic motivation grows.

4. Language Ego

Learning a new language involves developing new ways of feeling, thinking, and acting. This can seem, for some people, like a new identity. This new and different self can evoke different feelings in different learners, or even different feelings in the same learner at different times. There could be feelings of freedom. Some learners find that they can express through a new language thoughts that may have been considered taboo or inappropriate in their native language and culture. Or sometimes, learning new expressions or idioms for joy or surprise or amusement is just plain fun! On the other hand, though, the language ego can take a negative turn. A common complaint among older language learners is that they feel like a baby—helpless and incoherent. For a learner who feels he or she is not doing well in acquiring the new language, feelings of failure and inadequacy are common, and can be crippling.

How can a good teacher help a learner to find a positive alter ego through the new language? Older learners can be actively taught the concept of "language ego," preferably via a discussion in their native language. This can lessen the shock of feeling like you're not yourself in the foreign language. Then, it is often useful to highlight the potential that an alter ego can bring. Perhaps learners can be encouraged to play and sing and have fun in ways that they might not let themselves do in their native language. Finally, sharing personal stories often helps. Nonnative-English-speaking teachers may have an advantage in this regard, as they can talk about their own English learning journey. All TESOL professionals should have experience in learning a second or foreign language, and these experiences can encourage ELLs. I share with learners how helpless I felt during my first year in Indonesia, when I was trying to learn the language and learn how to live there. Students then can see the teacher as a safety net for their feelings of discouragement, and as a mentor who will show them the way to their proficient new language ego.

5. Self-Confidence

One factor at play in language ego is self-confidence. When learners have more confidence to begin with, their self-preservation resources won't dwindle as quickly when the trials of language learning begin to wreak havoc on their self-esteem. Successful language learners are self-confident language learners. They believe that they can achieve their language learning goals, and this fundamental belief carries them through the hard times.

However, it is important not to overestimate the staying power of self-confidence. Learners sometimes begin a course of study with a great deal of motivation and self-confidence, but quickly lose it if they believe their language learning to be unsuccessful. I have spoken with individuals who had great enthusiasm and motivation when they moved to a new country. Yet 5 or 10 years later, some have not acquired the new language as they thought they would, and express frustration and defeat. Their initial self-confidence was sometimes worn down through ineffective teaching—teaching that they did not know was ineffective, having never learned about SLA. By and large, ineffective learning opportunities were not named as the culprit. Rather, the blame was internalized, leading these once confident and capable individuals to believe that they were simply "bad language learners." Many ended up returning to their home countries or retreating to their native language communities in defeat.

How can a good teacher ensure that self-confidence is maintained and developed in his or her learners? Positive reinforcement goes a long way. We need to find what students are doing right, and where they are being successful, and point it out. When a student speaks and makes a mistake, we can applaud the willingness to speak. When a student writes, we can point out 10 errors instead of 50, and help the student to successfully correct those 10.

It is not enough to be a cheerleader, though. Self-confidence is probably most damaged when the language that students hear is not at the i + 1 level of comprehensibility, as we learned about in Chapter 4. Instead, perhaps the language students hear is at i + 5, or i + 20, or i + 83. Nothing deflates language learning confidence more quickly than continually being incapable of understanding anything. Requiring language work of students that is too difficult for them to accomplish successfully is probably the most common way in which teachers rob students of their self-confidence.

6. Risk-Taking

Successful language learners are willing to make mistakes. They are willing to take risks, and therefore they have more opportunities to learn through both successes and failures. Unfortunately, teachers sometimes do not encourage risk-taking. When only the "right" answer, or only a "correct" utterance, meets with approval, students quickly come to learn that guesses and feeble attempts are not welcome. Soon, the only voices heard are of those who already know the answers or who already have good language skills. Everyone else—especially the ELLs who need speaking practice the most—has been silenced.

Risk-taking is an especially tricky issue because it is so cultural. Different societies have different views of trial-and-error approaches to learning. When incorrect responses are linked to loss of face and shame, little risk-taking is likely to occur. How can a teacher respect cultural differences but still encourage risk-taking? Though there is certainly no simple solution, these tactics can sometimes be helpful:

a. **Discuss the need for risk-taking in language class.** If possible, this discussion should take place in the native language, or at least in the ESOL classroom. Students may never have thought of risk-taking as a language learning strategy. Thinking of it in this way can increase willingness to try. At the same time, by framing it primarily as a language acquisition strategy, any perceived critique of the culture is diminished.

b. **Elicit corrections until success is achieved.** If a response is incorrect, provide scaffolding until the student can produce a correct response. As this becomes commonplace in the classroom, students realize that the teacher will ensure that they are successful.

c. **Set students up for success.** This may involve providing opportunities to produce language that you know is easy for students, at least at first, as students are finding their voices. It may also involve giving a particularly skittish student advance notice that he or she will be called on in class, so he or she can prepare a response and be ready.

d. **Use group and pair work.** When students work in smaller groupings, they are speaking in front of fewer people, and are more willing to take risks. As you gradually create larger groups, students can become more accustomed to taking risks in producing language no matter who is listening.

7. Native-Language Effect

A learner's native language can both facilitate and interfere with learning the new language. Words that are similar in both languages (cognates), will help in language learning through what we call transfer. Features that are different, however, may hinder the language learning process through interference. For example, as a learner of Indonesian, I could easily learn the word *buku* because it was similar to the English word *book*. This cognate provided easy transfer from my native language to my new language. However, learning the word *nanas* for *pineapple* proved to be much more difficult. The fact that it shared similarities with the word *bananas* interfered with my ability to purchase the fruit that I wanted at the market! Transfer and interference occur with structures as well. Spanish speakers learning English may put an adjective after a noun, for example, as that is where it goes in Spanish.

How should an understanding of the native-language effect steer a teacher of ELLs in his or her choice of methodologies or strategies? First, we should not underestimate the impact of the native language. It is the language template that is known, and the target language will be viewed in relation to it. This is not necessarily bad. Our native language knowledge helps us a great deal in understanding structure, word formation, grammatical possibilities, and so many other concepts. Still, there are several things we can do to address the native-language effect:

a. **Discuss interference head-on.** If we know words or structures in the native language that will cause confusion for ELLs, we can help students through direct instruction on these items. We may say, for example, "Notice where the adjective goes in English. Is that the same or different from Spanish?" We should help students actively notice these differences.

b. **Utilize cognates.** Teach with cognates when you can. It is especially helpful to use cognates with beginners. One of my favorite lessons to use with older beginning language learners is on geography. As I weave the names of many countries and geographical locations into my lesson, students invariably recognize the country names, and thus can follow what I am saying. They can understand more of the target language than they thought they would be able to, and self-confidence is increased and stress is diminished.

c. **Understand language distance.** Languages vary in their similarity with one another. We say that two languages that share many cognates and similar structures have little "distance" between them. Such is the case, for example, between Spanish and Portuguese. Languages which are quite dissimilar, on the other hand, have a large distance between them. This becomes important in our schools as we notice that, for example, a Vietnamese learner is struggling much more with the English language than a German student. Though there could, of course, be many reasons for this, one is no doubt the greater language distance between Vietnamese and English.

8. Interlanguage

All language learners go through a developmental process during which time they use the language imperfectly. The language that students use during this process has been called their interlanguage. It is by its very nature flawed, but a learner's interlanguage should be seen as progress, not as errors.

Understanding the concept of interlanguage can be helpful for both learners and teachers. Learners can benefit from thinking of errors as marking progress rather than deficit. If the language were not being used, errors would not be made. Teachers can assure learners that trying to use new words and structures, even if the usage is imperfect, is good, and signals that language acquisition is taking place. Teachers can benefit from a learner's interlanguage by using it to guide teaching. How students use the language shows us what they know and don't know, or what they can use with ease and what they lack fluency in.

A caution about interlanguage: it should not be mistaken for fossilization. Sometimes, a learner gets stuck at a certain level of competency, either in general or in specific skill areas, structures, words, or sounds. If a learner continues to make the same errors over a significant time period, and the errors are not diminishing, language growth in that area has stopped, and fossilization has set in. Fossilized patterns of language use are extremely difficult to change. It behooves us as teachers to ensure that we teach for *accuracy* as well as for fluency, to try to prevent error fossilization.

■ ■ ■ Characteristics of Effective Classrooms

A teacher who is well prepared to foster English language acquisition and who understands learner needs is well on his or her way to creating the kind of classroom that will result in language acquisition. For example, he or she may ask more open-ended questions, provide a longer wait time for responses, and configure small groups for maximum ELL participation, because he or she understands the importance of risk-taking and self-confidence. Still, the teacher will need to choose from among many different types of methods for instruction. Should he or she use a PowerPoint or a reading? Will he or she give a quiz or pair work for review? This next section provides four qualities of good classroom activities, as guidance for selecting instructional methods.

Classes Should Be Meaningful

We know that students have more motivation, lower stress levels, more investment, more willingness to engage, and greater learning overall when classes are meaningful to them. Even the most dedicated student may have difficulty remaining alert and engaged while memorizing lists of unrelated words, studying grammar rules, or reading an article about something he or she does not find interesting. When engaged with topics and activities that are personally meaningful, on the other hand, students don't have to continually draw on sheer willpower to stay engaged. The topics are relevant. The activities are enjoyable. Relationships are built, and the student is making friends by engaging in the tasks assigned.

To illustrate, consider an ESOL class where the goal is to learn how to give directions. In class A, a textbook map is used, and students are formulating sentences to help a fictitious textbook character get from the library to the park. In contrast, class B does not have a textbook. Instead, the teacher has drawn a map of the part of the city in which their school is situated. Now, students are giving directions for Sylvia, a student in the class, to go from the school to the variety store around the block. In class A, students are only learning language. In class B, students are learning language, finding out where things are located in their community, and building relationships.

Meaningfulness also has to do with the topics chosen for reading, writing, speaking, and listening tasks, and how relevant those are to the students. For example, a reading on animal rights may be of interest to those living in areas where there have been related controversies, but may seem absurd and even offensive to individuals who have come from parts of the world characterized by human suffering.

Teachers of content areas such as math, science, and history of course have their content largely prescribed. Still, teachers can make many choices to increase the meaningfulness of that content, especially for ELLs. For example, the study of ancient Mayan culture in history class could have particular relevance for students in the classroom who have come from Mexico.

Learning Should Be Authentic

The activities in the classroom should, as much as possible, be authentic. That is, they should be more like real life and less like school. Authenticity does not often characterize our classrooms. Where else but in classrooms do we hear so many display questions— questions that the questioner knows the answer to? A history teacher might ask, for example, "Who was the first president of the United States?" Presumably, the teacher already knows the answer. A more genuine question might be "Which of the founding fathers do you think took the most risks?" A question asking for an opinion will almost always be genuine, as we don't know the students' opinions before they give them.

Questions are not the only application for authenticity, however. Tasks, things that we ask students to engage in during class, can also be authentic or not. A task is authentic when it either is or mirrors a real-world activity. For example, consider the three tasks below that are all designed to help students learn and practice months and numbers in a beginning ESOL class:

1. Students are matching numeral cards with their corresponding number words.

2. Students are putting the months in the correct order on a worksheet.

3. Students are going around the room and asking their classmates for their birthdays.

Which task demonstrates the most authenticity? You have probably correctly identified #3. Asking for and giving birthdays is a real-world activity, and it is useful for students to develop automaticity in giving their birthday, as well as in listening and writing down the dates given by others. What about the first two activities? Do they have any place in language learning? Certainly. These tasks could introduce language and provide some initial opportunities for practice. However, very often traditional lesson activities such as matching, copying, and ordering are not used to prepare learners for the eventual authentic task that they will engage in, but are rather ends in themselves. A good approach when designing lessons for maximum language and content learning is to ask yourself, "What is the authentic task that I want to prepare students to do?" Then, select scaffolding activities to prepare students for success in the final task.

Classroom Experiences Should Be Interactive

It probably comes as no surprise that learners need to interact, both with each other and with the teacher, in order to learn language. You may recall the sociocultural perspective, which emphasizes the importance of human interaction in language acquisition. We have also learned about risk-taking, and how it can be encouraged through small group work, and how stress may be lowered through pair or group work. Interaction is good and necessary in the classroom—for both language and content learning. Perhaps the most important reason ELLs need to interact is so that they have opportunities to develop oral language by speaking with each other.

An additional reason, though, is that we hope our classrooms will become learning communities—places where learners know each other, support one another, and strive to help each other learn. This can only happen if learners are provided sufficient interaction time. As an example, let's look at a class in which students are learning reported speech. They are learning to transform a sentence like "Adam said, 'I will go'" to "Adam said that he would go." The teacher could have students transforming sentences on a worksheet, working silently and independently. Or the teacher might divide the class into two groups. Each group is tasked with getting individuals from the other group to present something at an upcoming talent show. Students go one at a time to the other group, to ask each person a question. They return to their home group to report, with statements like "Mario said he would play his violin" and "Lana said she would bring cookies." Students have not only practiced the target structure, they have done so by interacting with each other and learning more about their classmates.

Learning Goals Should Be Framed as Tasks

The final learner-centered characteristic that we will discuss here is most commonly referred to in TESOL as task-based language teaching. This is an approach to language teaching which sets out a target task for students to complete, often in groups, with the assumption that students will use and develop certain kinds of language on the way to the completion of the task. It is inherently more motivating than viewing language use itself as the end goal. For example, imagine that Argentina is being studied in social studies class. The teacher wants students to know all the main imports and exports, the population, the location, and the capital city. Instead of just assigning this as simple memory work, a task might be "Prepare to interview tomorrow for the exciting position of ambassador to Argentina!" ELLs know they need to not only know the facts, but also practice stating them. Students learn the same content, but for a purpose, rather than as an end in itself.

Some writers on task-based language teaching say that a task in language classrooms is defined by its real-world nature. That is, completing a grammar worksheet is not what we mean by a task because it is not something that is typically done in the real world. A language acquisition task might be writing an email to someone, or identifying family members in a picture, or filling out a job application. Others say that tasks do not have to be real world—that is, some classroom tasks qualify. Such tasks might include identifying the differences between two pictures, or writing a paragraph about someone you admire.

No matter which definition of task we choose, tasks provide structure and goals in language learning, and in content classes as well. They often increase motivation, as students can see beyond the classroom to how the language, knowledge, and skills they are learning in school transfer to real life.

■ ■ ■ What Is K–12 Language Acquisition Called?

You will have noticed throughout this chapter that we now talk much more about how language is learned than how it is taught. It is no accident that this shift in perspective mirrors the shift away from learning language in language classrooms to learning language in content classrooms . . . while learning math, science, music, and all other content areas of a K–12 education. In recent years, there has been increased interest in content-based language teaching, extending beyond K–12 settings. Also called content and language integrated learning, this approach to language acquisition emphasizes learning other content, such as math, science, cooking, or sports through the medium of the target language. Methodologies within this approach vary in terms of how much the target language is actively taught. Sometimes this approach is used by content instructors who may understand little about language acquisition and who may assume that the target language will be learned incidentally as the focus of the classroom remains on the content. We know, however, that incidental language learning does not sufficiently develop language skills for most students. Some focus on the language itself is needed.

Immersion education can be thought of as full-time content-based language teaching. This is what most children learning English in English-medium K–12 schools experience. Students of all ages, through university and even beyond, in professional development settings, may learn all or most of their academic content through a language in which they are not yet proficient. The term immersion education often refers to 100% immersion in a foreign/second language academic context. However, the immersion concept can also be found in partial immersion situations, where perhaps 80% of the school day is in the target language and the other 20% in the native language. Children can learn a target language well through immersion, if the language and content is scaffolded well to provide comprehensible input. Sometimes, this is not the case, and students in immersion settings actually experience what has been called submersion . . . full immersion in a school language that is not sufficiently altered to provide comprehensible input. Submersion experiences typically result in a great deal of frustration for both learners and teachers, and limited effective language acquisition.

In the bilingual education model, students experience some immersion and some native language instruction, in an academic context. Though the varieties of bilingual education are too numerous to explore here, one highly effective model is dual language instruction. In this type of bilingual education, children receive instruction through both the target language and the native language in roughly equal amounts, though content is not duplicated. Often, a school of this type seeks equivalent numbers of native-speaking children from each language group. Dual language instruction has been found more effective than other childhood language acquisition models in some of the research (Collier & Thomas, 2004). Whereas immersion education may result in the loss of the native language, and may not produce highly proficient second language users, dual language models are much less likely to experience these negative results.

It is important to remember that content-based language teaching, immersion, and bilingual education are not new concepts. For centuries, children in many parts of the world have only had access to education through a nonnative language—a reality that continues in some places today. So, learning a language while acquiring academic content is not a new phenomenon. What is relatively new is the intentional choice of such schooling options for the main purpose of language acquisition. Parents today in Indonesia or Germany or Uruguay may choose full or partial English immersion schools for their children not because good educational opportunities do not exist in their native languages, but because they believe this is the best English-language acquisition opportunity for their children. Likewise, English-speaking parents in Canada may choose French immersion schools for their children as the most effective way for them to acquire both national languages. In the United States, dual language Spanish, Mandarin, Japanese, and other language programs are becoming increasingly popular.

Conclusion

The significant increase in the recent past in parents who actively choose K–12 schooling as the primary vehicle for their child's English language acquisition is both exciting and challenging. It is exciting to see language acquisition efforts expand beyond the boundaries of traditional English language classrooms. But it is at the same time inherently challenging to have two equally important goals to achieve during every class session: language and content learning. Hopefully, this chapter has provided some of the keys to ensure the achievement of these goals, by developing the teacher, student, and classroom qualities that are essential to success.

GRAB AND GO!

Go to **www.tesol.org/school-leaders** to access the Grab and Go links and downloads for this chapter.

How Does Someone Learn English in School?

1. K–12 schooling is an optimal place and time to acquire an additional language. However, a school context that fosters language acquisition requires intentionality. ESOL classes, content classes, leveled placement, and curriculum all work together to provide a rich environment for language acquisition. Hire well-qualified TESOL professionals who can orchestrate these various dimensions of a successful ESOL program.

   - Ensure that the ESOL teacher is a TESOL professional who has the appropriate communicative competence, linguistic knowledge, theoretical knowledge, and methodological competence to teach ELLs at all levels of proficiency.

   - Ensure that the TESOL professional has a key voice in decisions pertaining to all aspects of the ESOL program.

2. The principles of language acquisition are relevant to all parts of the school day, in all classrooms and social venues. Ensure that all teachers and staff understand the principles of language acquisition.

   - Provide school-wide professional development on the principles of language acquisition. See **Brown's Principles of Language Acquisition** online.

3. All teachers need to create classroom environments in which the content is meaningful, and the classroom experiences include authentic, interactive tasks.

   - Provide school-wide professional development on creating meaningful, authentic, and interactive learning tasks.

   - Provide opportunities for the TESOL professional to collaborate with content teachers to ensure that classroom activities are good learning experiences for ELLs at various proficiency levels.

4. There are a number of different models for acquiring a new language during K–12 schooling. Be familiar with the model used in your school, and what is required for effectiveness.

   - Read about the various models in this chapter.

   - Work with your TESOL professional to ensure that your chosen model is implemented well.

◼ ◼ ◼ References

Brown, H. D. (2007). *Teaching by principles: An interactive approach to language pedagogy* (3rd ed.). White Plains, NY: Pearson.

Callahan, R. M. (2013, February). The English learner dropout dilemma: Multiple risks and multiple resources. *California Dropout Research Project: Policy Brief 19*. Retrieved from http://www.cdrp.ucsb.edu/pubs_reports.htm

Collier, V. P., & Thomas, W. P. (2004). The astounding effectiveness of dual language education for all. NABE Journal of Research and Practice, 2:1. Downloaded Retrieved from: http://hillcrest.wacoisd.org/UserFiles/Servers/Server_345/File/Publications/ELL /Dual%20language%20survey.pdf

Dormer, J. E. (2011). Teaching English in missions: Effectiveness and integrity. Pasadena, CA: William Carey Library.

Harmer, J. (2015). *The practice of English language teaching with DVD* (5th ed.). Harlow, United Kingdom: Longman.

Olsen, L. (2014). Meeting the unique needs of long-term English language learners: A guide for educators. National Education Association. Retrieved from https://www.nea .org/assets/docs/15420_LongTermEngLangLearner_final_web_3-24-14.pdf

CHAPTER 6

::

Where Can an ELL Best Acquire Language and Learn Content?

School leaders are often excellent planners. We can devise programs and schedules that look great on paper. But then, students enter the picture. And what was neat and straightforward suddenly becomes very messy. Exceptions start popping up everywhere. Needs arise that were not expected. Student realities are different than those envisioned at the planning stage. And suddenly, we feel as if we're back to square one. The reality is that nothing is ever simple and straightforward when dealing with real, flesh and blood, individual students. And this is especially true of English language learners (ELLs). The richness and diversity that ELLs bring into our schools translates into very diverse and individualized needs.

Schools, as well, have different realities in terms of programmatic possibilities. Numbers of ELLs, budget constraints, and the local context will all affect decisions on how ELL needs are met. In this chapter, we first look at factors affecting ELL needs, then we discuss language levels and assessment, and finally we look at some possible programmatic models for ensuring that ELLs can thrive both in language and academic development in our schools.

▨▨▨ Factors to Consider in ELL Placement

You may have noted that the title of this chapter refers to "an ELL" and not "ELLs." It is rare for a school to have a significant number of ELLs whose needs are identical and who can be lumped together for planning purposes. ELLs will need *individualized* learning plans. This section addresses the various ways in which ELLs differ.

Home Language and Culture

Most ELLs are initially identified through a home language survey (see example in Appendix B). Given to any family suspected of speaking a language other than English at home, this survey is the starting point for the information needed about an ELL. (See sidebar about problems associated with the home language survey.) However, it is only a starting point. Take the scenario of a home language survey returned to the school indicating that a child has come from Kenya and speaks Swahili at home. This information should prompt us to try to discover much more. Is the child from a well-educated family in Nairobi, with parents whose English language skills are equivalent to yours and mine? Or has she grown up in a refugee camp in Kenya with limited formal schooling, with parents who originally came from Somalia, and who actually speak a mixture of Swahili and Somali at home? The language learning and schooling needs for each of these children would be very different.

Many children have multiple languages in their backgrounds. Some come from countries where many different languages are spoken, having perhaps one dominant home language but several other languages with which they are familiar. This could be the case for many students from Europe, Asia, and Africa. Sometimes children have multiple languages in their background because they have moved a lot. Perhaps a child is born to Japanese parents, in Hong Kong, and attends a smattering of different Japanese-, English-, and Chinese-medium schools. This child has an impressive language background to draw on.

What cultural background or backgrounds is the child coming from? Recalling the Flower Model of Culture from Chapter 1, we know that the "roots" of culture, values and beliefs, are not visible. We may see that a Muslim girl wears a head covering, for example. But this outward expression of culture and religion doesn't tell us if she comes from a cultural background in which girls have equivalent academic opportunities as boys, or one with low academic expectations for girls. Such cultural differences have a tremendous impact on the child's (and family's) adjustment to our way of schooling and our values. As another example, we may be aware that Koreans typically place a very high value on education, and may thus assume that parents will be happy to have their child receive additional language support. We may be surprised, then, to find ourselves facing a distraught father who believes that his family has lost face by having a child placed in what he perceives as a "remedial" class like ESOL. It is important to try to tease out the unique linguistic and cultural backgrounds that students bring with them, so that we can know best how to use their strengths and predict their challenges.

Problems in Identifying ELLs

The home language survey is not a foolproof system for identifying students in need of ESOL services. Sometimes, parents do not want their children in ESOL programs, and falsely state that English is the language used at home. Other times, non-English-speaking children are recent arrivals to an English-speaking home—whether through adoption, foster care, international student status, or a move to stay with English-speaking relatives. In still other situations, the language spoken at home is not English, but the child is not an ELL, or is at a high English level, and is best served in regular classrooms. The home language survey is a good starting point, but should not be the sole basis for placement.

Previous Education

A child's previous level and type of education is of utmost importance as well. Two children may have identical levels of English. But if one experienced good prior education in his home country and language, and the other did not, there will be significant differences in their needs. Many research studies have shown that children with strong first language development have a significant advantage in second language development (see, e.g., Cummins, 1981). This is one reason why it is so important to encourage continued use of the native language at home.

First language development often goes hand in hand with schooling in the first language. It is no surprise that children coming from strong educational systems in their own countries will likely master the new language, given sufficient time, and suffer no long-term loss in language or academic content. The outlook for those coming from poor educational backgrounds is not as promising. They may be facing an overwhelming number of "firsts" in our schools, including some or all of the following:

- First exposure to the Roman alphabet
- First exposure to learning-focused, as opposed to final exam focused, schooling
- First exposure to activities intended to build critical thought, such as questioning and small group work
- First exposure to some content areas, such as higher level math, or American history

- First exposure to a school focus on learners as individuals, with the expectation of self-regulation rather than group control

In addition to these potential firsts, which may be experienced by many ELLs, some children may be coming from backgrounds where they did not have adequate schooling, and may be considered students with limited or interrupted formal education. These students have educational needs that go beyond English language needs, and which must be considered in providing them with a good program for language and academic learning.

Aptitude and Interest

All children vary in aptitude for different subjects, and in interest in them. But we sometimes fail to recognize and utilize such differences with our ELLs because we are so focused on language. ELLs will, like any other population of learners, be more motivated by subjects that they enjoy than by those that they do not. So, it behooves us to know if an ELL is particularly good at art, for example, or loves math, or finds history incredibly boring no matter what language it comes in. Such information becomes a piece of the placement puzzle. For example, let's say an ELL has just come from Honduras, and is at a beginning level in English. In your school's plan, he is to be out of core content subjects, learning English with other newcomers in the ESOL classroom, for the first month. This is a good plan for some students. However, you discover that he loves science, and is particularly fascinated by how things work. You know that his grade-level science class is currently studying cell phone technology. Where is this child best served? His interest and aptitude for science may well dictate a change of plans during science period, placing him back in the regular classroom, to glean as much as he is able from the highly visual and experience-oriented science classes that his teacher has planned. This student may not need to be fluent in English to grasp the cell phone technologies being taught in science class. Having success in science class may be all the motivation he needs to learn more English. He could take visuals and models back into the ESOL class, where the teacher could use them as a basis for building his language skills.

And what about language aptitude? While many people believe that some individuals are "good at language" and others aren't, this is a dangerous and unsubstantiated perspective. Though individuals may differ in their ability and interest in tasks such as learning grammar rules or memorizing vocabulary, such activities are not part and parcel of learning to communicate in a new language. Language learning is very complex, and different learners may experience it differently. Nonetheless, *everyone* is capable of learning a new language, and this is the mindset that all teachers should have with regards to school-aged ELLs. Further, language mastery is not required for learning academic content through a language. Imperfect command of the English language should never prevent access to academic content and learning.

Classroom Contexts

It is not only the ELL characteristics that must be considered in placement. The classroom environments themselves must be taken into consideration, too.

Where regular content classrooms are concerned, we might consider the following:

- How large is the class? Is the teacher likely to have time to address the needs of the ELL?

- How effective is the teacher in teaching language? Has the teacher been trained to help ELLs with language development, and has the teacher taken ownership of that goal?

- How effective is the teacher in teaching content to ELLs? Does the teacher modify her speech appropriately? Does the teacher use many visuals, hands-on experiments, and group and pair work? Is the teacher warm and caring?

- What are the other students like? Do they embrace other languages and cultures as "cool," and take a genuine interest in students from other countries? Are they empathetic and helpful when working with ELLs in class groupings? Is there anyone in the class who speaks the first language of the ELL and who is willing to help the ELL?

Where ESOL classes are concerned, we might consider the following:

- How effective is the ESOL teacher? Is he or she a TESOL professional? Does he or she have a track record of helping students make significant gains in language through focused ESOL classes?

- How much time does the ESOL teacher have for each student? Are there other students in the ESOL classroom that will take precedence for the teacher's time, relegating the ELL under consideration to work alone or in front of a computer?

- Does the ESOL teacher have the authority, materials, and skill to provide the ELL with the kind of language instruction that he or she most needs during ESOL classes, or is the teacher tasked with preparing students for tests or helping them with homework from content classes?

Language Level

Finally, we come to the most important factor of all: language level. How much English a child is able to speak, understand, read, and write really is the driving force behind decisions about placement. Beginners, those who know little or no English, really do have no more pressing task than to get a basic grasp of the English language. This "basic" English has been called "social English" or, as we saw in Chapter 4, basic interpersonal communication skills (Cummins, 2000). This foundational language is necessary simply for survival in an English-medium school. An ELL needs to, as quickly as possible, be able to ask for and understand answers regarding important places and activities in the school, learning such language as how to ask to go to the bathroom, and how to comprehend announcements given verbally and in writing. We saw in Chapter 4 that stress inhibits language learning, and there is nothing more stressful than an environment in which nothing is understood.

Because it is so crucial for beginning ELLs to acquire that important foundation of social language as quickly as possible, schools should adopt a "whatever it takes" attitude toward facilitating this initial language acquisition. The older the learner, the greater the chances that basic interpersonal communication skills will be best developed through significant time with a TESOL professional, before expecting the student to engage and produce in academic content classes.

Though the acquisition of social language lessens stress and provides the foundation for further language learning, it is only the beginning of a very long journey. A frequent misunderstanding is that because a student sounds fluent in informal conversation, he or she is therefore equipped to participate fully in academic coursework. Nothing could be further from the truth. According to many experts (see, e.g., Cummins, 2000; Collier, 1989), social language can be acquired well in 1–2 years, while it takes ELLs 5–7 years to catch up to native speakers where academic language is concerned. So, a big part of the answer to "where can ELLs best be served" is in knowing where they can best develop academic language, even as they begin to learn academic content through the new language.

■ ■ ■ Understanding Language Levels

There are many ways to describe language learner proficiency levels. The words *beginning,* *intermediate,* and *advanced* are often used as rough indicators of language proficiency. These are sometimes placed alongside a 5-level progression, with the beginning level sometimes referred to as "Level 1" and advanced as "Level 5" (see Figure 1). Beginning levels can also be referred to using the term "raw beginner" for students who do not know any of the language, and "false" beginner for those who believe themselves to be beginners, but who actually know some basic language such as numbers 1–10, the alphabet, and common phrases such as "What is your name?" and "How are you?" Because English is so prevalent around the world, "false beginners" are common in ESOL classes. At the other end of the spectrum, it is important to realize that even advanced learners, especially those who are older, often know many fewer words, idioms, and expressions than native speakers.

TESOL International Association Level Descriptors

TESOL International Association's level descriptors for its *Pre-K–12 English Language Proficiency Standards Framework* (2006) can provide a useful overall understanding of the progression of language acquisition. These are provided here:

Level 1—Starting

At Level 1, students initially have limited or no understanding of English. They rarely use English for communication. They respond nonverbally to simple commands, statements, and questions. As their oral comprehension increases, they begin to imitate the verbalizations of others by using single words or simple phrases, and they begin to use English spontaneously. At the earliest stage, these learners construct meaning from text primarily through illustrations, graphs, maps, and tables.

Level 2—Emerging

At Level 2, students can understand phrases and short sentences. They can communicate limited information in simple everyday and routine situations by using memorized phrases, groups of words, and formulae. They can use selected simple structures correctly but still systematically produce basic errors. Students begin to use general academic vocabulary and familiar everyday expressions. Errors in writing are present that often hinder communication.

Level 3—Developing

At Level 3, students understand more complex speech but still may require some repetition. They use English spontaneously but may have difficulty expressing all their thoughts due to a restricted vocabulary and a limited command of language structure. Students at this level speak in simple sentences, which are comprehensible and appropriate, but which

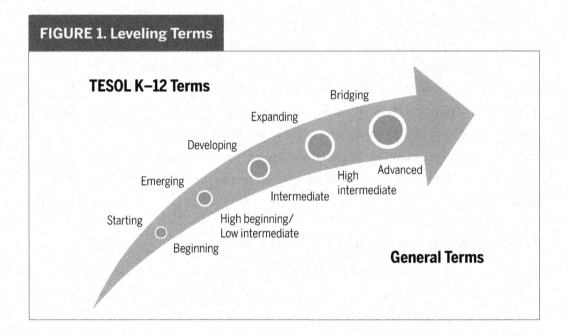

FIGURE 1. Leveling Terms

TESOL K–12 Terms

Bridging

Expanding

Developing

Emerging

Advanced

High intermediate

Intermediate

Starting

High beginning/
Low intermediate

Beginning

General Terms

are frequently marked by grammatical errors. Proficiency in reading may vary considerably. Students are most successful constructing meaning from texts for which they have background knowledge upon which to build.

Level 4—Expanding

At Level 4, students' language skills are adequate for most day-to-day communication needs. They communicate in English in new or unfamiliar settings but have occasional difficulty with complex structures and abstract academic concepts. Students at this level may read with considerable fluency and are able to locate and identify the specific facts within the text. However, they may not understand texts in which the concepts are presented in a decontextualized manner, the sentence structure is complex, or the vocabulary is abstract or has multiple meanings. They can read independently but may have occasional comprehension problems, especially when processing grade-level information.

Level 5—Bridging

At Level 5, students can express themselves fluently and spontaneously on a wide range of personal, general, academic, or social topics in a variety of contexts. They are poised to function in an environment with native speaking peers with minimal language support or guidance. Students have a good command of technical and academic vocabulary as well of idiomatic expressions and colloquialisms. They can produce clear, smoothly flowing, well-structured texts of differing lengths and degrees of linguistic complexity. Errors are minimal, difficult to spot, and generally corrected when they occur (pp. 3–4).

■ ■ ■ Assessment

Terminology

If there is one area of education in which school leaders are usually well versed today, it is assessment. The increasing demands for data, accountability, and reporting have resulted in assessment-driven systems and programs. Still, it may be helpful at the outset to ensure a common understanding of assessment terminology. We will begin with three main terms: assessment, evaluation, and testing.

Assessment is an overarching term that usually simply means collecting or finding evidence of what a student can do. It is often used to mean ongoing assessment, which is why it is the term associated most with regular monitoring of progress within the classroom. Ongoing, classroom-based assessment can also be called formative—assessment that is for the purpose of "forming," or teaching, the student.

Evaluation is another overarching term. It is often used in connection with judging or interpreting the evidence that is collected. For example, a teacher may evaluate evidence in order to give a grade. Evaluation is often linked to summative assessment, referring to an evaluation at the end of a course of study, rather than ongoing (formative) assessment for the purposes improving teaching and learning. To summarize:

- *Formative assessment* "forms" the student throughout the course.
- *Summative evaluation* "sums up" the learning at the end of the course.

A final word that is used in multiple ways is *testing*. This is sometimes also used interchangeably with *assessment* and *evaluation*. In reality, however, tests are one type of assessment—a type that is frequently used for the purpose of evaluation. Tests are often used for summative purposes. Standardized testing, the use of official tests to gauge achievement, introduces us to yet another term: normative. A norm-referenced test will show how a particular student compares to others. Such tests are often used to determine an English proficiency level.

Purposes

There are three main reasons why we assess students' language proficiency. First, we may assess language proficiency for placement purposes. When a student comes into our school system, we need to know where he or she will best be served in learning English and academic content. The language placement test is a crucial piece of that puzzle.

Second, we assess students for the purpose of ascertaining their progress. When a teacher gives a test after a unit of instruction, she intends to discover whether students have indeed made the learning progress that she expected. Simpler measures of progress are daily, informal checks. After learning and practicing a new structure for a class period, for example, a teacher may fill out an informal assessment checklist as he listens to students using the new structure. The checklist is intended to help him document whether students have indeed mastered the new language, or whether reteaching or more practice is needed.

Finally, we provide assessments to measure achievement. After a semester in ESOL class, for example, what language has been acquired?

Qualities of Assessments

There are many different ways in which assessments can be measured to determine their degree of effectiveness. We will look at four of these here: validity, reliability, practicality, and washback.

An assessment is considered valid if it measures what it is intended to measure. For example, if a teacher has just taught past tense forms and wants to see if students have learned what she has taught, she may design a simple fill-in-the-blank test asking students to provide the past forms of verbs. This may be valid if the teacher wants to assess this passive knowledge. However, what if this teacher's goal was actually that students be able to use past tense forms in real communication? If this was the teacher's intent, then we would say that the fill-in-the-blank test is not the most valid assessment, as it does not measure students' communicative use of past tense forms.

Reliability has to do with the degree to which we can depend on the results. That is, we look at the likelihood that the test will produce the same results every time. Reliability is a very important factor in high-stakes testing, but much less so in ongoing, formative classroom assessment.

Practicality is a quality that needs no explanation. Language assessments vary in how practical they are to conduct, and given the fact that all educational systems have time and financial constraints, practicality is an important consideration. Practicality must be considered in conjunction with the purposes of assessment. When assessing students for placement, we generally want a system that is quick and efficient. We may want to use a simple multiple-choice test, for example, in conjunction with a short oral interview. With a high-stakes achievement test, on the other hand, practicality yields to validity and reliability in importance.

The final quality of language assessments that we will discuss is washback: the effect of assessment on instruction. Washback can be either positive or negative. If the assessment system is such that it promotes the achievement of the learning goals, then washback is positive. For example, imagine that a goal for beginners in an ESOL class is to be able to ask directions of school personnel about how to get to various places in the school. If students are assessed on this ability through a classroom simulation of a dialogue with the school secretary, for example, the washback would be positive. Students would be accomplishing the learning objective as they prepare for the assessment.

Washback is frequently negative, however. Imagine the same classroom as described in the preceding paragraph. Only this time, the assessment at the end of the course is a written test emphasizing grammar, spelling, and vocabulary forms. Because students and teacher know they need to prepare for this test, precious class time is spent on grammar, spelling, and vocabulary—not on developing the communication skills to interact with school personnel. The goals are not met in this case precisely because of the negative washback of the final test.

Performance Assessment

After this brief introduction to assessment in general, we will now zero in on the kind of ongoing, formative assessment that is most helpful for developing language skills: performance assessment. Performance, in this case, simply means that students will use language, and that teachers will assess how well they perform as they read, write, speak, or listen in English. Whole books and courses are devoted to performance assessment, so we certainly cannot cover it in depth here. However, we will look at three components of classroom-based language assessment that can be effective: performance tasks, student involvement in assessment, and portfolios.

Performance tasks

We have seen the word *tasks* used quite a bit in this book, most notably in task-based language teaching. When teachers take a task-based approach to language teaching, they provide learners with tasks that involve them in using the language, most often simulating or actually engaging in real-world language use. After students have had opportunities to acquire language through tasks, they can then be asked to perform very similar tasks for assessment purposes. Any activity that requires students to use language that they have learned, demonstrating communicative competence for the purpose of assessment, is a performance task. The advantages of performance tasks over more traditional types of assessment such as pen and paper tests are obvious: Students are assessed on real communicative ability rather than on passive language knowledge. Performance tasks are as varied as the teachers who create them. They can be relatively simple, such as assessing students' ability to introduce themselves by stating their name, where they live, and what they do or study. Or this fairly simple task could be one in a series of small tasks leading to a larger performance task, such as engaging in a simulated job interview.

Performance tasks are often evaluated using rubrics. Let's look at a possible rubric for the performance task mentioned above: engaging in a simulated job interview. This kind of performance task might be appropriate for ELLs in high school. After students have learned pertinent language and information about job interviews, and after they have had opportunities to engage in at least one simulated job interview as practice, the teacher could then set up an interview as a performance task, for the purpose of assessment. The teacher might even invite a colleague to come to class and play the role of the interviewer, leaving himself free to assess student performance. The teacher might use a rubric such as the one shown in Table 1. As the student engages in the task, the teacher evaluates the performance in each of the four categories shown on the left. Each receives the number of points in accordance with performance, as shown across the top, for a total of 10 possible points.

Because rubrics bring clarity to what is expected in performance, and specificity in how students can improve, they help teachers align instruction to assessment, and help learners understand how they can improve.

Informal, formative assessment also can also include daily or weekly checks on progress. Usually, such informal assessment does not involve a detailed rubric like the one in Table 1. Rather, the teacher may fill out a simple chart like the one shown in Table 2, while listening to students performing a task.

Whether formal or informal, extended or brief, performance assessment tasks allow teachers to look for evidence of communicative competence in real student language use, rather than in passive knowledge.

Table 1. Rubric for Interview Performance Task

	Points: 0–.5	Points: 1–1.5	Points: 2–2.5
Introduction and qualifications for job	Student needs to improve in 2–3 of these areas: • Gives name and other pertinent personal information • Tells about pertinent education • Tells about pertinent experience	Student needs to improve in 1–2 of these areas: • Gives name and other pertinent personal information • Tells about pertinent education • Tells about pertinent experience	Student excels: • Gives name and other pertinent personal information • Tells about pertinent education • Tells about pertinent experience
Cultural appropriateness	Student needs to improve in 3–5 of these areas: • Friendly and positive • Dressed appropriately • Asks questions and shows interest • Uses appropriate forms of address • Is neither boastful nor reticent	Student needs to improve in 1–2 of these areas: • Friendly and positive • Dressed appropriately • Asks questions and shows interest • Uses appropriate forms of address • Is neither boastful nor reticent	Student excels: • Friendly and positive • Dressed appropriately • Asks questions and shows interest • Uses appropriate forms of address • Is neither boastful nor reticent
Answering questions	Needs to improve in 2–3 of these areas: • Answers questions promptly • Uses "stall" techniques as appropriate • Uses mostly positive responses	Needs to improve in 1–2 of these areas: • Answers questions promptly • Uses "stall" techniques as appropriate • Uses mostly positive responses	Student • Answers questions promptly • Uses "stall" techniques as appropriate • Uses mostly positive responses
Language	• Student has frequent errors in grammar, word choice, or pronunciation • Errors hinder communication Describe errors:	• Student has some errors in grammar, word choice, or pronunciation • Errors occasionally hinder communication Describe errors:	• Student has few errors in grammar, word choice, or pronunciation • Errors do not hinder communication at all.

TOTAL: ___ / 10

Table 2. Informal Acquisition Checklist

Linguistic item being assessed: _____

Date	Student	Student has significant difficulty	Student has some difficulty	Student shows mastery

Student involvement in assessment

Because learning a language can really only be done by the student, it is helpful to involve students in assessing their progress. Teachers can facilitate not only language acquisition, but also their students' ability to assess and moderate their own learning. Students should be able to identify signs of learning, note weaknesses and areas for improvement, and set learning goals.

There are many tools that teachers can utilize to help students do this. Students can keep learning logs—notebooks in which they record their daily learning, or charts provided by the teacher to note learning activities, degree of success, and further goals. Learning logs can be a useful part of a self-evaluation scheme in which learners formally assess their learning periodically in the course. Such more formalized self-assessment may even contribute to the grading scheme.

Journals can also be utilized in a multitude of ways to involve students in assessment. They may be an expanded form of learning log, written in narrative rather than note form, thus improving writing skills as well as inspiring self-reflection. Journals can be shared between teacher and learner. Such journals are sometimes called dialogue journals. This type of journal involves students in assessment as teachers pose questions such as "What did you learn today?" or "What can you do to improve in your pronunciation?"

Reflections are another common writing task that involves students in their own assessment. Students can reflect on interactions in English outside the class, their level of success in their academic content classes, their feelings about the language acquisition process, their speculations on activities they could engage in to progress faster—any number of reflective issues or topics relating to assessment could be addressed. Though we often think of reflection as occurring as a written task, reflection can occur orally as well. When two students dialogue on issues such as those listed above, they can reflect on and assess their own learning.

Portfolios

A final performance assessment tool that is particularly effective for language acquisition is the portfolio. A portfolio is a collection of items, sometimes called artifacts, which demonstrate language acquisition. Portfolios may be for the purpose of demonstrating progress, in which case they generally show work at various stages, and highlight the progress that has been made. Portfolios can also be for the purpose of showing achievement. Such portfolios do not show progress over time, but rather focus on the student's current ability.

Whatever the focus and goal, portfolios provide students with an opportunity to show their performance—how they can actually use the language. Artifacts of student writing have in the past been the easiest to include in portfolios. However, with the option of online portfolios, audio and visual files demonstrating oral skills are just as easy to include. Other artifacts could be visual representations of learning, such as a chart showing transfer and interference between the native language and the new language. Or students may want to include pictures representing successful communication moments in the community, such as a photograph of them with a store clerk, accompanied by a brief written description of the interaction.

Portfolios are usually most successful in documenting performance and engaging students in assessment when guidelines such as the following are in place:

1. There is a limited number of artifacts (usually under 10), and they meet specific guidelines correlated with the learning goals.
2. Students must include an introduction to the portfolio as well as an explanation of each artifact.
3. Students must include a summary reflection on their learning.
4. The portfolio must be attractive and inviting.

It is important to understand that everything in this section on performance assessment can work together. In my school in Brazil, students kept a portfolio, and regularly assessed themselves after performance tasks (see Dormer, 2010).

Cultural Factors

No discussion of assessment in TESOL would be complete without addressing the issue of culture. First, we need to realize that our students will have perspectives about assessment, evaluation, and testing that come from their cultural backgrounds. Whether it is a belief that pen and paper tests are the only valid form of measurement, or that students cannot possibly participate in their own assessment, cultural perspectives are important in considering the issue of assessment. Rather than dismissing student opinions when they clash with best practice in TESOL, we should engage in respectful dialogue.

Students are not the only ones bringing cultural expectations to the issue of assessment. Standardized testing has increased in many of our schools. As a result, many teachers, as well, may view these "official" types of tests as the only ones with validity.

Another cultural issue in testing is the content of the tests—especially on standardized tests. It is easy to underestimate the degree to which cultural background can impact our understanding of words and situations. Consider the scenario of a student who has recently arrived from Jakarta, and who lives in an apartment building in an urban area. The student reads this question on a standardized test:

Which of these items would NOT be in a yard:

a. A barbecue

b. A TV

c. Grass

d. A dog

First, the student may never have seen an American-style yard. Second, the student may envision dogs as dirty pests that roam the city. He may be aware that some people keep them as pets, but may reason that, if this is the case, the dog would be kept inside. Finally, he may picture the outdoor entertainment area of his apartment complex in Jakarta, which includes a TV. So, he may come to the conclusion that *d* is the correct response. This question likely was designed to show whether or not the student knew the meaning of the word "yard." The student did have an understanding of "yard" as an outdoor living space, but lacked the cultural background to select the correct choice to demonstrate his understanding.

Though teachers can't be expected to know what cultural barriers students from many different countries and backgrounds may face with regard to the content of standardized tests, simply developing an awareness of this issue can help teachers to see standardized tests in a new light, and to be on the lookout for potential culture-based misunderstandings.

Standardized Testing

We have already seen, above, that once students are in our schools, their progress in language acquisition is often best facilitated by performance assessment, rather than standardized tests. However, standardized testing can be beneficial for placement when students first enter school, and in many places is regularly mandated to show yearly progress.

It is beyond the scope of this book to discuss mandated testing procedures or resources in detail, as those vary from context to context. However, the WIDA (World Class Instructional Design and Assessment) system is worth mentioning, because of its widespread adoption in the United States and internationally. WIDA has worked closely with TESOL International Association, and many school districts have adopted or adapted TESOL's *PreK–12 English Language Proficiency Standards*. Many also use WIDA's testing system for both placement and progress. See more about WIDA here: https://www.wida .us/standards/eld.aspx.

▪▪▪ Program Models

Any effort to prescribe in theory where an ELL should be placed is dangerous, as there is no such thing as a theoretical student! All students are unique, bringing a myriad of differences like the ones discussed at the beginning of this chapter. Still, school leaders need some basis on which to design models and suggest guidelines, programs, and schedules.

A rule of thumb for most learners, in most contexts, is this: ELLs should always be in grade-level content classes *if* they have the necessary language, background, and support to learn the content in those classes.

This may seem pretty straightforward, but it can be difficult to ascertain what the "necessary language, background, and support" actually is for various subjects, at various grade levels, for students from diverse backgrounds. The placement issue is further complicated by the current trend to "push in" to regular classes at all costs. In other words, in many schools there is a belief that students can benefit from most academic content classes no matter what their language level or background. In this section, we will discuss some program model factors, and types and trends, and we will end with a suggested placement template.

Regular Content Classes

Throughout this book, I have suggested that regular content teachers should all be trained, willing, and able to do two things for ELLs who are at intermediate language level proficiency and above:

1. Further language development

2. Teach content

Sometimes, regular teachers are expected to meet the language and content needs of ELLs who are at low beginning levels. When the ELL is in upper elementary through high school, this is often an unrealistic expectation. Teachers may respond to this untenable situation by trying to teach beginning ELLs, possibly diverting teaching time from higher level ELLs and students who are fully English proficient. In worst-case scenarios, a teacher's frustration in trying to meet the needs of beginning ELLs may cause the teacher to resist teaching *any* ELLs. So, expectations placed on regular content teachers need to be realistic, recognizing that the older the ELL who is coming into the school with no English, the more likely he or she needs the kind of English language development that a TESOL professional is trained to provide.

Sheltered Classes

Sheltered classes are academic content classes which are tailored to the language needs of ELLs. In many ways, they are the ideal solution for schools with significant numbers of ELLs, as they can be designed to meet language, culture, and content needs. For example, a sheltered 8th-grade American history class would ensure that

- the language used by the teacher and in texts is comprehensible to ELLs;
- the background knowledge needed for the content is provided in the course, rather than assumed;
- continued language acquisition is equal to content learning in course goals; and
- the curriculum standards are met.

Because sheltered classes have the potential to enable ELLs at lower language levels to meet grade-level curriculum standards, while not neglecting their language development, they are without a doubt one of the best programmatic choices for schools with a high number of ELLs. A well-known resource for the development of sheltered classes is Sheltered Instructional Observation Protocol (SIOP; see http://siop.pearson.com/ and http://www.cal.org/siop/).

Coteaching

A fairly recent trend is to have a TESOL professional and content teacher co-teach together in a content classroom (See Honigsfeld & Dove, 2012). This can be an effective model, especially when older ELLs have limited English. Some challenges with this model, however, are the TESOL professional's limited time with each student when there are many ELLs at different English levels in the class, the time needed for collaboration, and the expense that is inherent in having two teachers in many classrooms. Still, when collaborative teaching is designed well, it can serve the needs of both ELLs and native speakers well, within content-area classrooms.

Programs for Beginners

Students who come to school knowing no or very little English may be placed in a variety of programs to develop basic language skill. Students are sometimes pulled out of content-area classes to receive basic ESOL instruction in the ESOL classroom. The older the student, the more likely that this foundational language learning is needed before the student is held accountable for content learning. For this reason, some schools or districts with a high number of ELLs have developed "newcomer" or "intensive English" programs. Such programs are extremely helpful for ELLs with very limited English at the high school level, when there is limited time to both acquire the language and accumulate the credits needed for graduation. Such a program might provide a semester of intensive English on academic/content topics before engaging in content subjects for high school credit. Or, it may be bilingual or multilingual in nature, keeping students on track academically through the native language while helping them to acquire English as quickly as possible. The term *newcomer* should be used with caution, however, as individuals could need this type of program even though they are not "new," and not all newcomers need this type of program.

ESOL Classes/English Language Development

The main function of ESOL classes should be English language development. Unfortunately, ESOL classes are sometimes viewed as a place where an ESOL teacher simply helps ELLs with homework in other content areas. This should not be necessary if content teachers are well-trained to work with ELLs. Instead, ESOL class time should be used for the important task of helping students to continue their English language development. Within ESOL classes, students at different language levels require different instruction. Unfortunately, sometimes all the ELLs in a particular grade level are pulled out and taken to the ESOL class at the same time, regardless of their differing language levels. So, the TESOL professional must teach the beginning ELL who arrived from Somalia just last week alongside a Hispanic student who was born in the United States whose English sounds native-speaker like, but who struggles with reading and writing—all in the same 40-minute period.

Students are best served by instruction that is geared to their language level, and this is especially true for beginners. The reality in many schools, however, is that scheduling dictates the same ESOL pull-out period for all the ELLs in a given grade. If this scheduling problem cannot be overcome, and if there is considerable diversity in language levels within a single period, the school should at least provide a qualified aid in the ESOL classroom.

Putting It All Together

A quality ESOL program in a school may very well have all of the above options, which students would experience at varied language and grade levels, according to their individual needs. In other words, a quality ESOL program has more than one way for ELLs to receive the language and content learning that they need. What is paramount is to ensure that ELLs spend the bulk of their school day in environments in which they are learning language and academic content simultaneously. This may mean time in an ESOL class or with an ESOL coteacher in a regular class for considerable periods of time during initial placement, with the student's individual program changing as he or she achieves basic English proficiency to time spent mostly in the regular classroom, learning both language and content from a teacher who knows how to help ELLs achieve both of these goals.

Students who do not yet speak any English should not languish in regular classrooms in which they understand nothing; but neither should students who have gained some English proficiency be kept out of advanced regular content classes simply because they are ELLs. Systems must be in place so that both extremes are avoided, and so that students can quickly learn foundational language and then have full access to all levels of academic content through the ongoing language support that well-trained regular classroom teachers can provide.

■ ■ ■ A Sample Placement Chart

Table 3, Sample Placement Chart, attempts to provide a snapshot of where ELLs at different language levels and in different grades might be best served. Of course, each student has individual needs and experiences, and this chart is only a generalization. It is important to realize that in most cases, even advanced learners are operating with significantly less language and cultural understanding than a typical native speaker. Therefore, it is imperative that *all* regular classroom teachers have training in second language acquisition, and view themselves as language teachers.

Key to Chart

Note: These terms are used in many different ways in different programs and by different authors. This key is not meant to define these terms, but simply to indicate their meanings on this chart.

Pullout = Student is pulled out of all major academic subjects (English language arts, math, science, social studies) to receive intensive English language instruction. Student remains in physical education, art, and music.

Partial pullout = Student is pulled out of language-dense subjects (English language arts, history) to receive sheltered instruction in these subjects.

ELA pullout = Student is pulled out of English language arts only, to work on specific ELL needs, especially related to the acquisition of academic language. (Note: in high school, the ESOL equivalent to the English language arts class should also receive English credit.)

Regular = Student is in the regular classroom, but with a teacher who knows how to modify and teach for language acquisition.

Sheltered instruction = Student is in content classes that are tailored for ELLs at his/her language level. Sheltered instruction *may* serve to provide the initial English language instruction needed by beginners. If the sheltered program is designed with this goal in mind, then it may serve as an alternative to "pullout." Note that sheltered instruction is part of the "partial pullout" designation as well.

Newcomer/intensive program = Older learners with very little or no English are placed in a special program that provides intensive language development, while being academically focused.

TABLE 3. Sample Placement Chart

	Level 1 Starting (Beginning)	Level 2 Emerging (High Beginning)	Level 3 Developing (Intermediate)	Level 4 Expanding (High Intermediate)	Level 5 Bridging (Advanced)
Kindergarten	Regular				
Grade 1	ELA pullout	Regular			
Grade 2	Partial pullout	ELA pullout	Regular		
Grade 3	Pullout or sheltered instruction*	Partial pullout	ELA Pullout	Regular	
Grade 4	Pullout or sheltered instruction*		Partial pullout Or ELA pullout	Regular	
Grade 5	Pullout or sheltered instruction*		Partial pullout Or ELA pullout	Regular	
Grade 6	Pullout or sheltered instruction*		Partial pullout Or ELA pullout	Regular	
Grade 7	Pullout or sheltered instruction*		Partial pullout	ELA pullout	Regular or ELA pullout
Grade 8	Pullout or sheltered instruction*		Partial pullout	ELA pullout	Regular or ELA pullout
Grade 9	Newcomer/ intensive program	Sheltered instruction and/or Partial pullout		ELA pullout	Regular
Grade 10	Newcomer/ intensive program	Sheltered instruction and/or Partial pullout		ELA pullout	Regular
Grade 11	Newcomer/ intensive program	Sheltered instruction and/or Partial pullout		ELA pullout	Regular
Grade 12	Newcomer/ intensive program	Sheltered instruction and/or Partial pullout		ELA pullout	Regular

* Sheltered instruction is always preferable to pullout, if the academic content can be provided at the child's language level, and if it provides for the foundational language acquisition that is needed at beginning levels.

Shaded area: Provide access to advanced academic courses.

Coteaching

Because coteaching models are so varied, this option is not reflected on the chart above. Coteaching may be an effective replacement for pullout models, in some instances, and sheltered instruction in others. However, care must be taken that the ELL's needs are actually met through the coteaching arrangement, whether those needs are for beginning language development alongside sheltered academic content, or for higher level language development while working with the regular course content.

Conclusion

The question of where to place each ELL, and how to overcome the barriers to optimal placement is arguably one of the most difficult that school leaders face in regards to ELLs. Even when school leaders understand well what an ELL needs, and have a strong desire to meet those needs, it is rarely possible to provide ideal placements at all times during each school day. My hope is that increased awareness of placement needs will lead to a greater percentage of the school day being spent in language and content learning environments in which ELLs can thrive.

GRAB AND GO!

Go to **www.tesol.org/school-leaders** to access the Grab and Go links and downloads for this chapter.

Where Can an ELL Best Acquire Language and Learn Content?

1. There are many factors to consider when scheduling classes for ELLs, including previous education, language level, and interests. Work with your TESOL professional to personalize each ELL's class schedule according to the student's particular needs.

    ■ Consider multiple sources of data, including the home language survey; language proficiency; educational background; and parent, teacher, and student input. See the **Home Language Survey** in Appendix B.

    ■ Ensure that the TESOL professional has a key voice in placement decisions.

2. ELLs at different levels of proficiency have vastly different needs. Provide learning experiences which address these different needs.

    ■ Personalize schedules for ELLs, rather than providing the same schedule for all ELLs in a specific grade.

3. All testing and assessment procedures need to take into account an ELL's language proficiency level.

    ■ Select appropriate resources and implement procedures for accurate language proficiency assessments.

    ■ Provide school-wide professional development on differentiating academic content assessments for ELLs.

4. There are a number of different types of classes that can meet the needs of ELLs for both acquiring language and learning content. Be familiar with concepts such as "coteaching," "newcomer/intensive" classes, and "sheltered instruction." Design an effective overall model, similar to the placement chart in this chapter, for your context.

    ■ Work with your TESOL professionals to identify the characteristics of your student and teacher populations, and design a placement model for your context.

    ■ Provide specific training for content teachers who may need to provide sheltered instruction or instruction for newcomers, or who may co-teach with a TESOL professional.

References

Collier, V. P. (1989). How long? A synthesis of research on academic achievement in a second language. *TESOL Quarterly, 23*, 509–31.

Cummins, J. (1981). The role of primary language development in promoting educational success for language minority students. In *Schooling and language minority students: A theoretical framework* (pp. 3–49). Los Angeles, CA: California State University, Evaluation, Dissemination and Assessment Center.

Cummins, J. (2000). *Language, power, and pedagogy. Bilingual children in the crossfire.* Clevedon, England: Multilingual Matters.

Dormer, J. E. (2010). I can! Bringing self-evaluation to a task-based syllabus for language learning success. In M. C. Coombe & A. Shehadeh (Eds.), *Task-based learning.* Alexandria, VA: Teachers of English to Speakers of Other Languages.

Honigsfeld, A. & Dove, M. (Eds.). (2012). *Co-teaching and other collaborative practices in the EFL/ESL classroom: Rationale, research, reflections, and recommendations.* Charlotte, NC: Information Age.

Teachers of English to Speakers of Other Languages, Inc. (2006). TESOL pre-K–12 English language proficiency standards framework. Alexandria, VA: Author. Retrieved from http://www.tesol.org/docs/books/bk_prek-12elpstandards_framework_318.pdf?sfvrsn=2

Professional Development Guide

▪▪▪ Part 1: Helping School Leaders Design Professional Development

The first part of this guide helps school leaders design professional development for all teachers. Ideally, this professional development could be provided by the TESOL professional on staff. This resource is simply an outline of what a day of professional development on meeting the needs of English language learners (ELLs) could look like. All the issues are addressed at length in the various chapters in this book, referenced for each topic.

Language Levels (see Chapter 6)

1. ELLs at different language levels require different programs.

2. Beginning ELLs, those who do not yet have the English language skills to communicate even on very basic topics, require English language development, usually provided through ESOL classes. The older the beginning ELL, the less likely he or she will be best served in learning basic English by being immersed in regular classrooms for the majority of the school day.

3. Intermediate to advanced ELLs can best develop the academic language that they need by remaining in regular classes where teachers are well-equipped to teach content and language learning.

Concepts About SLA (see Chapters 4 and 5)

1. It is a myth that children simply pick up languages easily. Teachers need to understand the reality that English language acquisition is a long and difficult process, regardless of the age of the learner.

2. Social language and academic language are very different. Cummins (2000) has labeled these different types of language as basic interpersonal communication skills, which take 1–2 years to develop, and cognitive academic language proficiency, which can take 5–7 years to develop. A child who sounds very fluent on the playground may still not have developed much academic language, and may still be in need of focused English language development.

3. All children benefit from maintaining and continuing to develop their native language. Teachers should always encourage parents of ELLs to maintain their first language at home, and to actively work to help their child develop this language, for example, by reading books in the first language at home.

4. The native language is a needed and helpful tool in acquiring the new language of English. Translation, bilingual books, labels and charts, and conversations with classmates in the native language can all assist students on the path to learning both English and academic content. It is rarely appropriate to ban the use of the native language in school.

Culture and Affect (see Chapters 1–3)

1. Everyone in the school benefits from an environment that is multilingual and multicultural in nature. ELLs are an asset for the whole school community, as they can raise awareness and broaden perspectives on language and culture.

2. Affect plays a significant role in language acquisition. Students need to feel acceptance in their new school environment, and demonstrating appreciation for new cultures and languages can increase feelings of acceptance and lower stress.

3. ELLs experience stress on many levels when coming into a new school environment in a new language. Some stressors may include testing, hours spent in classrooms where nothing is understood, and disapproval of the use of the native language. We know that stress reduces language learning potential. Therefore, steps should be taken to reduce stressors wherever possible.

The Two Learning Goals of the ELL (see Chapters 5 and 6)

1. First, ELLs must acquire the English language in school. They do not acquire full proficiency in English *before* they can begin to learn content through the medium of English. However, it is important not to underestimate the importance of acquiring a foundational level of English as quickly as possible, upon arrival in an English-medium school.

2. The majority of the ELLs' time in our school, he or she will be learning academic content while simultaneously continuing to learn the English language. It is for this long-term task that all classroom teachers need to be well prepared.

Sheltering Academic Content (see Chapter 6)

1. Sheltering academic instruction is the concept of providing content in a way that is accessible for students who do not yet have full command of the English language. All teachers who have ELLs in their classrooms need to have a basic skill set for doing this.

2. Basic skills that all teachers need in order to shelter instruction include:

   a. The ability to convey concepts through multiple means, such as graphics, photos, experiments, reenactments, and role-plays.

   b. The ability to design effective interactive learning tasks, and the understanding of where to place ELLs in order to maximize their learning through pair and small group work.

   c. The ability to speak slowly and clearly, and understanding the importance of conveying information in more than one way, such as by writing, saying, and modeling instructions.

   d. The ability and willingness to modify texts and assignments as needed, in view of the ELL's language level.

Teaching for Language and Content Learning (see Chapter 5)

1. All teachers need to view themselves as language teachers. Native-English-speaking students are developing academic language through regular classes, just as ELLs are. So, it is helpful for all teachers to consider how they can help all students develop in reading, writing, speaking, and listening, through their subject area.

2. Teachers need specific strategies for helping intermediate and advanced ELLs to develop academic language (cognitive academic language proficiency) in their regular classes. Some of these strategies include:

   a. Adding language objectives to lesson plans. The regular addition of this component to all lesson plans will help all teachers to begin thinking about how they are overtly seeking to develop language skills in their classes.

   b. Identifying language items that are uniquely well-suited for development in a given content area, and then including these language items in learning tasks. For example, the content area of history provides many opportunities to comprehend and use various past tense forms. Math classes might provide opportunities for learning to use *if-then* structures, as they appear frequently in word problems.

   c. Providing ample time for students to use academic language in speech. ELLs, in particular, need opportunities in pair or small group work to formulate and speak complex sentences, aided appropriately by their peers.

   d. Understanding the need for both fluency and accuracy in language development. The additional talk time suggested above can help to develop fluency. Where accuracy is concerned, it is often appropriate for classroom teachers to work with ELLs for a few minutes in class individually, while other students are occupied with a task, to increase accuracy. For example, a student who says "I live in United State" may benefit from having a teacher work with him to elicit the correct statement "I live in **the** United State**s**."

3. Schools should acquire resources to help teachers identify specific ways that they can help ELLs learn both language and their specific content. There are texts and other resources that are content specific, such as books on teaching social studies or math to ELLs. There are also more broadly applicable lesson design resources, such as cognitive academic language learning or the Sheltered Instruction Observation Protocol.

■ ■ ■ Part 2: A Resource to Help Teachers Engage in Professional Development to Meet the Needs of ELLs

The second part of this guide is written for teachers. It simply lists ways that classroom teachers who are not trained in TESOL can create an optimal language and content learning environment for ELLs.

Dispositions

1. **Genuinely care about your ELLs.**

   Why:

   - Students are more motivated by a caring teacher than any other factor.
   - It is part of who we are and what we do as teachers.

   How:

   - Use their names (and say them correctly!)
   - Greet them in their native language(s).
   - Find out the cause of any "abnormal" behavior, such as not wanting to go to lunch (perhaps the student doesn't like American food) or not having homework done (perhaps the student has to take care of younger siblings at home).

2. **Build a classroom culture that appreciates linguistic and cultural diversity.**

   Why:

   - All students will benefit from a multicultural perspective.
   - ELLs will feel more like a part of the class, and more valued.
   - Native English speakers will get a glimpse of the difficulty of learning a language, and develop more empathy.
   - ELLs will benefit by learning some content vocabulary in their native language.

   How:

   - Encourage greetings and some other usages of the ELLs' native languages. (E.g., Let the ELL teach the class numbers in Chinese in a math class, and use the Chinese numbers when referring to exercises or pages; routinely use greetings and partings in other languages.)
   - Use other languages and cultural symbols on the walls. (E.g., Have maps of the various countries of the students in the class; give ELLs a place to post key academic words in their native languages alongside the posting in English.)

3. **Develop empathy for ELLs: Truly place yourself in their shoes.**

Why:

- Just caring about a student does not automatically result in empathy.
- It is not easy or natural to understand people who are very different from us; it requires conscious thought processes.
- We cannot adequately meet the needs of students whom we do not understand.

How:

- Ask yourself, "Would I understand this if it were in Spanish?"
- Ask yourself, "How would I feel if I spent all day in another language?"
- When giving homework, ask yourself, "Would I be able to do this in a foreign language that I don't know well?"

Perspectives

4. **Understand language levels: Beginning, intermediate, and advanced ELLs all have vastly varied language abilities.**

Why:

- Comprehension of any content provided through language requires "comprehensible input"—language that is at a language level that a student can understand.
- When ELLs are treated as a homogeneous group, typically the beginning and advanced students do not receive what they need—teachers tend to teach to the middle. The beginners often understand very little, and content learning suffers; the advanced students do not get the upper level language development they need, and never achieve college-ready language proficiency.

How:

- Use the TESOL *PreK–12 English Language Proficiency Standards* (2006) to know what the ELLs in your class can do, and don't expect more or less than they are capable of.
- Watch the ELL. Look for signs that he or she is not receiving comprehensible input:

- ☐ Silence—not talking in class
- ☐ Copying from a neighbor; plagiarism
- ☐ Falling asleep or a posture of apathy
- ☐ Overreliance on dictionaries or electronic translators
- ☐ Misbehavior

- ■ Talk to ELLs; have them show you how much they understand through specific tasks such as underlining all the words they don't know in a paragraph, or telling you how much time a homework assignment took them. This requires good rapport with the student, so he or she doesn't fear losing face, and will provide honest feedback.

- ■ Respect the "silent period" of beginning ELLs. Students typically need to listen for several months before they are ready to speak.

5. **Know the difference between social and academic language.**

Why:

- ■ ELLs can sound very fluent and communicate successfully in social contexts, and yet have very low academic language skills. (On the other hand, some international students may have greater control over academic language, and need to develop social language skills.)

- ■ Both social language and academic language are needed in order for ELLs to participate in the school community and flourish academically. When either is lacking, teachers need to address the gap.

- ■ Typically, social language develops in 1–2 years, while academic language can take 5–7 years.

How:

- ■ Don't assume that students who sound fluent have equivalent language capabilities as native speakers.

- ■ Use a Universal Design (See the Universal Design for Learning website: http://www.udlcenter.org/aboutudl) approach to teaching, so that ELLs who are still acquiring academic language can access the content.

- ■ Continue to differentiate homework and assessments for students who sound fluent.

Action

6. Use visuals.

Why:

- ELLs do not have the cultural and linguistic background knowledge that native speakers have.

- Pictures, charts, graphs, and other visuals or manipulatives can convey meaning without words, or can support the words that are used.

- Visuals do not detract from anyone's learning; they make the classroom more enjoyable for native English speakers as well.

How:

- Always ask yourself, "Is there a visual that could support this word, phrase, or idea?" For example, if making a reference to George Washington, a quick picture on a PowerPoint, captioned "George Washington, our first president" would be helpful.

- Think of possible misinterpretations that can be alleviated through visuals. For example, an ELL might hear "river bed" and be visualizing a bed in a river—a mental confusion that could result in the ELL missing the next several minutes of speech. However, if a picture of a river is shown as the teacher says "river bed," there is no confusion, and the ELL can focus on grasping the main idea of what is being said.

7. Use pair and small group work.

Why:

- ELLs can sometimes learn language and content better from their peers than from the teacher.

- Positive small group experiences can help the ELL to fit in socially.

- Small group work provides the ELL with much-needed opportunities to speak.

How:

- Teach all students how to do small group work. Don't expect them to automatically be able to work together in a multicultural group.

- Provide specific roles and tasks for each person in the group.

- Ensure that the ELL has a valued role in the group.

- Minimize lecture in favor of discovery learning in small group settings. This kind of teaching benefits everyone.

8. **View yourself as a teacher of content *and* language.**

Why:

- Even if you only teach native speakers, you *are* a teacher of language and content. All students learn the majority of the academic language that is needed for college readiness in content-area classes.

- Actively teaching language does not detract from, but rather adds to, the learning of content. Understanding of content is greater the more accurately students can talk and write about important concepts and ideas. Even words that native speakers may not use incorrectly, such as definite and indefinite articles, can provide opportunities for critical thinking and language development for all.

How:

- Focus in class on language items that can benefit all. For example, a history teacher might pause after reading "Gettysburg was a turning point in the Civil War; nevertheless, the end had not yet come." The teacher could ask students to write this down, leading them to understand the punctuation required for words like "nevertheless." The teacher could then ask students to think of synonyms or substitute phrases for "nevertheless." This kind of language development is needed by all, not just ELLs.

- Focus individually, with the ELL, on language that can be learned through your content area. For example, a math teacher might point out the repeated words "if" and "then" in a series of word problems, helping the ELL to understand that this is one way we talk about cause and effect. Similarly, the following sentence in a textbook "The treaty was *a* concern, but it wasn't *the* major concern . . ." could be followed by a discussion with the ELL on the difference in meaning between "a" and "the."

- Use ELL writing as a means to further language learning through feedback and corrections. However, be careful to assess the ELL only on content knowledge, not language skill.

9. **Build oral skills.**

   Why:

   - Research shows that in language immersion contexts (where students learn a language through their schooling), oral skills are typically not developed sufficiently.

   - ELLs often do not have ample opportunities to speak in class—either to the class as a whole, or in small groups. Sometimes this is simply because they lack the confidence to speak out. Other times it is because they lack the language. Either way, it is a problem to be addressed. Language output is *required* for full language development.

   How:

   - Teach native-English-speaking students how to interact with ELLs in small group work. Teach them about concepts such as wait time (allowing sufficient time for another student to respond) and scaffolding (supplying words or phrases that an ELL may be lacking, but still allowing that ELL to speak).

   - Never ask "Does anyone have a question?" Instead, ask "What questions do you have?" Requiring everyone to have a question allows the ELL to ask a basic comprehension question while encouraging critical thinking for the native speaker.

   - Provide a question in advance for an ELL. For example, say "Tomorrow I will call on you in class to answer this question. . . . You can prepare your answer tonight."

10. **Encourage use of the native language.**

    Why:

    - Research shows that developing the native language *always* increases the potential for learning a second language.

    - It is incredibly exhausting to only use a language in which you lack full proficiency all day long, and to not use your native language at all. Ask yourself if *you* could do that!

    - Using the native language can help students understand content better.

    How:

    - If you have several students who speak the same native language, provide them with opportunities to talk through the content in their native language. For example, they could reproduce a chart or a graph related to the content, in their first language.

- ■ Encourage students to keep vocabulary lists of academic words, so that they can learn the new terms in their native language as well as in English.

- ■ Add words, charts, graphs, and other visuals, in other languages, to bulletin boards and other spaces, alongside the English versions.

■ ■ ■ References

Cummins, J. (2000). *Language, power, and pedagogy. Bilingual children in the crossfire.* Clevedon, England: Multilingual Matters.

Teachers of English to Speakers of Other Languages. (2006). *PreK–12 English Language Proficiency Standards.* Alexandria, VA: Author.

APPENDIX A

Acronyms in TESOL

Acronym	Meaning	Usage
BICS	Basic Interpersonal Communication Skills	Cummins' (1979) description of social language
CALP	Cognitive Academic Language Proficiency	Cummins' (1979) description of academic language
EAL	English as an Additional Language OR English as an Academic Language	Replacing "ESL" in some contexts; the dual meanings occasionally cause confusion
EAP	English for Academic Purposes	Often used for secondary and postsecondary study that is specifically oriented toward preparation for university studies in English
EFL	English as a Foreign Language	English learning in countries which do not have English as a national or dominant language; English is typically learned as a foreign language subject in school
ELL or EL	English Language Learner or English Learner	Used to refer to students of English, especially in ESL contexts
ELT	English Language Teaching	Can be used to refer to the field of study, as in "a conference on ELT"; more prominent in EFL contexts
ENL	English as a New Language	Replacing "ESL" in some places, in recognition that for many students English is not a second, but a third or fourth language
ESL	English as a Second Language	English learning in countries which have English as a national or dominant language; English is typically learned by children in school or by adults in programs for immigrants

ESOL	English to Speakers of Other Languages	A term that can be used instead of both "ESL" and "EFL"; thus, it is increasingly used when speaking of all English learning contexts
SIOP	Sheltered Instruction Observation Protocol	An instructional planning and observation template for sheltered instruction
TEFL	Teaching English as a Foreign Language	Can be used to refer to the field of study, as in "Certificate in TEFL"
TESL	Teaching English as a Second Language	Can be used to refer to the field of study, as in "Certificate in TESL"
TESOL*	Teaching English to Speakers of Other Languages	Used to refer to the field of study, as in "Master's degree in TESOL"
TOEFL	Test of English as a Foreign Language	An English test that is usually taken by foreign students to gain entrance into American universities
ZPD	Zone of Proximal Development	Vygotsky's (1978) theory that development happens through interaction with a more proficient interlocutor

*Note that *TESOL International Association* is an international professional organization of English teachers, based in the United States. It is sometimes referred to simply as "TESOL," and it stands for Teachers of English to Speakers of Other Languages.

References

Cummins, J. (1979). Cognitive/academic language proficiency, linguistic interdependence, the optimum age question and some other matters. *Working Papers on Bilingualism, 19*, 121–129.

Vygotsky, L. S. (1978). *Mind in society.* Cambridge, MA: Harvard University Press.

APPENDIX B

Home Language Survey

Note: This survey should be provided in the parents' native language, or should be orally translated.

Student: _____

Age: _____ **Grade:** _____

Parent(s)/Guardian(s): _____

Information About Student

Family name (surname): _____

First and other name(s): _____

Date of birth: _____

Place of birth: Country: _____ State: _____ City: _____

Language used most often by student at home: _____

Other languages used by student: _____

Write what language the student typically uses for each of these activities:

Talking with mother: _____

Talking with father: _____

Talking with siblings: _____

Talking with other family members:

Family member: _____ Language: _____

Family member: _____ Language: _____

Family member: _____ Language: _____

Interacting with neighbors: _____

Interacting in the community (for example: shopping, playing sports, attending religious services, etc.)

_____

Watching TV: _____

When did the student first enter a school in which all subjects are taught in English? _____

What school did the student attend last year, and where is the school located? _____

Has the student ever been in a bilingual or ESOL program? ☐ Yes ☐ No

If yes:

For how many years? _____

Did the student exit the ESOL program? _____

Is the student here on an international student visa? _____

Information About Parent(s)/Guardian(s) in the Student's Primary Residence

Name: _____ Relationship to student: _____

Country of birth: _____

Language most frequently used within the home: _____

Language most frequently used with the student: _____

Name: _____ Relationship to student: _____

Country of birth: _____

Language most frequently used within the home: _____

Language most frequently used with the student: _____